Girma Bishaw is the director of the Gratitude Initiative UK, an organisation dedicated to promoting gratitude as a transformative practice in society. His work includes supporting churches on the margins, particularly diaspora churches, helping them engage more deeply with the wider mission in partnership with host churches. Girma has previously served as Co-director of The London Project and as a church pastor, contributing to the planting of several diaspora churches across London and the UK. He is married to Yodit, and they have a son and a daughter.

'You might think the topic of gratitude would constitute light reading about how to be a polite, generally pleasant individual. You'll soon find yourself thinking again, and again. Dr Girma Bishaw connects the absence of gratitude with diverse communities at an impasse and starkly divided nations. An appreciative approach to life grows when people trade a sense of entitlement for a posture of humility, a critical spirit for an eye that appreciates beauty. Prepare to be captivated, not only by Girma's story and research, but by gratitude itself as you never considered it … until now.'
Ellen L. Marmon, Ph.D., Professor of Christian Discipleship, Former Director of the Doctor of Ministry Program Asbury Theological Seminary

'Many of us think we understand gratitude, but Girma's book blows our previous understandings out of the water. He powerfully and prophetically articulates why gratitude is the essential posture for thriving communities today. Drawing from a depth of reflection, research and lived experience, he powerfully presents gratitude as the best framework for reconciliation and community cohesion.'
Andy Frost, Director at Share Jesus International, Chair at Mission Collective, Joint CEO for Gather Movement and the author of many books

'In *The Gratitude Way*, Girma Bishaw invites us to rediscover gratitude as a God-given approach to life in all its fullness. We are encouraged to embrace the perspective of gratitude as a framework for how we interact, which will resource us both to discern how to deal with questions of injustice, and to become destiny providers for those we encourage through our gratitude. Dr Girma prescribes gratitude as a gift that can heal and equips us with tools to accompany him on the way.'
John Tasker, Lay minister in the Diocese of London, a Commissary of the Bishop of Angola, and a trustee of MANNA and Mission Africanus

'Girma is my friend and as I've walked with him in good and hard times, I can say without exaggeration that Girma is one of the most beautiful souls I've ever known. That's because he embodies what this book is about: gratitude as a way of life. By blending together his personal story, biblical reflection and pastoral application, Girma has given us all a much-needed primer on why and how we can become people whose lives are marked by gratitude. Read, enjoy and watch God fill you with gratitude!'
Revd Dr Bijan Mirtolooi, Senior Pastor, Redeemer West Side, New York City

'Girma Bishaw, in *The Gratitude Way*, calls upon us to reject an increasingly angry world of resentment and to cultivate thankfulness as a means of God-given grace. The fruit of this endeavour is greater mental fortitude, wellbeing, altruism and compassion as we grow in mutual flourishing and solidarity. *The Gratitude Way* challenges a prevailing culture of negativity and encourages us instead to enlarge our sympathies. It offers a better way and I commend it to you.'
Rt Revd Christopher Chessun, Bishop of Southwark, Church of England

'This timely book is a precious gift, containing riches for the common good; an inspired, refreshing counter-narrative, blending theoretical discourse, intimate story-telling and humour to draw us into an expansive embrace of gratitude and harvest benefits for ourselves and release positive change in the world around us.'
Revd Dr Jacqueline McLeod, Senior Pastor, Living Word Christian Fellowship

'Girma is a winsome and convincing advocate for gratitude's power to transform people, relationships and society. What a difference it would make if we embraced his counter-cultural message to lead change through gratitude with truth and grace.'

Dr Tracy Cotterell, Project Faculty, Portland Seminary; Senior Mission Associate, London Institute of Contemporary Christianity

'Girma Bishaw's *The Gratitude Way* reveals how the power of developing the spirit of gratitude in our lives is transforming not only for us as individuals but for the societies in which we live.'

Revd Dr Allan Barth, Vice President of Redeemer City to City, Global Catalyst for Europe, Middle East and Africa

'Girma Bishaw makes a radical proposal that has the potential to make the world a better place for us all. Gratitude is the balm that heals our world and the oil that transforms our societies. His message is clear, his tone is persuasive, and his stories are engaging. We ought not only to thank God for the gift of one another. We must be grateful for us all – we can only be fully human when we are in communion with others who are different from us.'

Dr Harvey Kwiyani, Chief Executive at Global Connections

'Those who spend any time with Girma will know that he himself is a gift from God, and that when it comes to gratitude he certainly practises what he preaches. This exploration of and apologetic for gratitude, from many angles and from multiple voices, will I hope stimulate both discussion and change, both personally and societally. I'm thankful for *The Gratitude Way* and recommend it.'

Dan Strange, Director, Crosslands Forum

'In my experience, it is rare to find a book that not only has obvious academic depth, engaging with a wide range of literature from philosophical, to sociological, psychological and theological, but which is also well applied and moving. With the mixture of personal anecdotes, stories, insights and your cross-cultural

perspective, the book manages to provide all that and more. It warmed my heart and has strengthened my commitment to "give thanks in all circumstances".'
Pete Nicholas, Senior Pastor, Redeemer Downtown, New York

'Girma Bishaw's *The Gratitude Way* is engaging, profound, challenging and practical. Girma makes a fresh and compelling case for the posture of gratitude, a posture that he himself embodies. In so doing, he creates hope for transformation. I highly recommend it.'
Revd Dr James Robson, Principal, Oak Hill College

'Revd Dr Girma Bishaw, in this ground-breaking book, *The Gratitude Way*, is providing a new framework for diverse societies to speak to one another and to bridge longstanding divides. In a polarised world, we need gratitude – acknowledgement of the good – more than ever. It is an important starting place, rooted in the gospel of Jesus Christ, that will bring us closer to Him and each other.'
Professor Anne C. Bailey, author of *The Weeping Time: Memory and the Largest Slave Auction in American History*

'We can't always change the circumstances and challenges in front of us, but we can choose our posture and response. In this great book, Girma outlines what a response born out of gratitude truly looks like and how this counter-cultural approach can profoundly impact our places, situations and relationships. I am so grateful for this significant book at this important time.'
Gavin Calver, CEO Evangelical Alliance

'In this book, Dr Girma Bishaw's writings reveal a man who not only passionately embodies his message but also adopts a prophetic stance on healing societies plagued by hatred, bitterness and racial division. He has found a language that empowers everyone to engage meaningfully in this pursuit, unpacking the "healing powers" of gratitude as both an antibiotic combating negative emotions and a vitamin strengthening resilience. Offering essential perspectives for a way of life that extends beyond individuals to families, communities and nations, this book is a must-read – whether you are a sceptic or a bearer of hope, a pessimist or an optimistic seeker of solutions for a world in turmoil.'

Revd Celia Apeagyei-Collins, President, The Rehoboth Foundation International

'I came to the United Kingdom in 1965. It is so easy to forget the good things that have happened to you and the people who have helped you through difficult times. This book has helped me to remember the teachers, the neighbours, my teenage friends, work colleagues and church leaders who have been so generous and kind in many ways over my many years of living in the United Kingdom. Thank you, Girma, for this book. It has been so helpful in making my heart consciously grateful.'

Revd Les Isaac OBE, Founder and President of Ascension Trust

INTER-VARSITY PRESS
SPCK Group, Studio 101, The Record Hall, 16–16A Baldwin's Gardens,
London EC1N 7RJ, England
Email: ivp@ivpbooks.com
Website: www.ivpbooks.com

© Girma Bishaw, 2025

Girma Bishaw has asserted his right under the Copyright, Designs and Patents Act 1988 to be identified as Author of this work.

All rights reserved. No part of this publication may be reproduced, stored in a retrieval system, or transmitted, in any form or by any means, electronic, mechanical, photocopying, recording or otherwise, without the prior permission of the publisher or the Copyright Licensing Agency.

Scripture quotations are taken from Holy Bible, New International Version®, NIV® Copyright ©1973, 1978, 1984, 2011 by Biblica, Inc.® Used by permission. All rights reserved worldwide.

Scripture quotations marked AMP are taken from the Amplified Bible. Copyright © 2015 by The Lockman Foundation, La Habra, CA 90631. All rights reserved.

Scripture quotations marked NABRE are taken from the New American Bible (Revised Edition). Scripture texts, prefaces, introductions, footnotes and cross references used in this work are taken from the New American Bible, revised edition © 2010, 1991, 1986, 1970 Confraternity of Christian Doctrine, Inc., Washington, DC All Rights Reserved. No part of this work may be reproduced or transmitted in any form or by any means, electronic or mechanical, including photocopying, recording, or by any information storage and retrieval system, without permission in writing from the copyright owner.

First published 2025

British Library Cataloguing-in-Publication Data
A catalogue record for this book is available from the British Library.

ISBN: 978-1-78974-596-2
eBook ISBN: 978-1-78974-598-6

Typeset by Fakenham Prepress Solutions
Printed in Great Britain by Clays Ltd

Produced on paper from sustainable forests

Inter-Varsity Press publishes Christian books that are true to the Bible and that communicate the gospel, develop discipleship and strengthen the church for its mission in the world.

IVP originated within the Inter-Varsity Fellowship, now the Universities and Colleges Christian Fellowship, a student movement connecting Christian Unions in universities and colleges throughout Great Britain, and a member movement of the International Fellowship of Evangelical Students. Website: www.uccf.org.uk. That historic association is maintained, and all senior IVP staff and committee members subscribe to the UCCF Basis of Faith.

THE GRATITUDE WAY: CREATING COMMON GROUND IN A DIVIDED WORLD

Girma Bishaw

Contents

Foreword – Rt Revd Dr Ric Thorpe, Archbishop of
   Melbourne   xii
Acknowledgements   xv

Introduction   1
1 My journey to this point   4
2 Why gratitude and why now?   12
3 Gratitude explored   34
4 Gratitude misunderstood   53
5 The biblical and theological foundation of the gratitude
   way   67
6 Gratitude and social change   94
7 The benefits of gratitude   111
Conclusion   131

Afterword – Ruth Naomi Floyd   137
Appendix 1: Learning to cultivate gratitude – some ideas   139
Appendix 2: Learning to cultivate gratitude – discussion
   topics   141
Appendix 3: Case study – Islington Gratitude Dinner   142
Further reading   146
Notes   147

Foreword

I have a confession to make. I love the idea of gratitude because it helps me appreciate the life I live. I like being around people who express gratitude – they are definitely more pleasant to be with. So, I always try to say thank you and look for opportunities to do so to express that gratitude. But I haven't reflected on gratitude much beyond that, and I have discovered that there are treasures waiting to be uncovered, relationships ready to be transformed, and challenging circumstances having whole new solutions being brought to bear. I have missed out on so much and I realise I am the poorer for it. If you think you know what gratitude is, I invite you to be challenged and have your mindset changed.

I first met Girma when he was a fellow minister in Islington. He is a kind, thoughtful, generous-hearted man, who loves sharing time over a meal, preferably Ethiopian, to find common ground and look for opportunities to do something together that will change life for the better. Every time I meet him, I come away feeling appreciated, listened to, encouraged and more hopeful. I have come to understand that this arises from a deep conviction that when you look for the good in someone else, call it out, and explore the depth and breadth of that good, it changes the relationship between us. To encounter this is to be profoundly impacted.

I experienced this first-hand when Girma asked me to help him organise a celebration event to enable 2,000 people from more than 100 nations who had made Britain their home to acknowledge and celebrate the best of Britain and the good things they had experienced and received by coming to the United Kingdom. At first, I took some persuading. After all, I knew that many from other nations and ethnicities had experienced racism and discrimination of various kinds. How could they prioritise acknowledging and celebrating the good when they had experienced such rejection and cruelty? But Girma was adamant. If you start by looking for the positives and celebrating them, it does not deny addressing the negatives, but rather changes the relationship and empowers different kinds of conversations that then lead to better outcomes. Girma expresses the good in such a way that it leads to wonder, new perspectives and a determination to address the negatives in a different and more life-giving way.

This approach is deeply challenging and deeply humbling. It is challenging because it is so counter-intuitive and runs against all my own expectations and prejudices. When I expect anger and hurt, and receive love and gratitude instead, I have to ask myself what is going on and dwell in that place of surprise and bewilderment. And it is humbling because I have to give up control over how I think this kind of interaction should go, and I am forced to confront myself and receive what is being offered generously and freely.

And I cannot force gratitude. It is totally in the hands of the one who expresses it, if it is to be genuine. But when it is expressed, something beautiful, something even supernatural happens because grace has come into the space between us. Life-giving opportunities emerge that draw us closer together. Miracles become possible.

So, gratitude becomes so much more than saying thank you. That is, of course, the most common expression of it. But there is so much more to it when we begin to discover its riches and it becomes a force for radical change and transformation. This book will take you on that journey of discovery where you can discover those riches for yourself. It takes a deep dive into the value and practice of gratitude, through Girma's own doctoral research, and includes a range of conversations with people who have reflected on gratitude for many years. It is rich and far-reaching in its application. If you embrace it, it will change the way you approach relationships, resolve conflict, and even appreciate everyday life. I commend Girma and this book to you.

Rt Revd Dr Ric Thorpe
Archbishop of Melbourne

Acknowledgements

The greatest gift to humanity is another human being. God reaches us through others, and it is only through the presence and contributions of those around us that we can truly reach our full potential. This has been profoundly true in my journey with the Gratitude Initiative and in writing this book.

From the very beginning, when the concept was fragile and in its infancy, I was blessed with people who took the time to listen, to understand what I was trying to communicate, and to encourage me forward. Their faith in me and their unwavering support have brought me to this moment.

I am especially grateful to the trustees of the Gratitude Initiative – Rt Revd Dr Ric Thorpe, Matt Bird, Dr Harvey Kwiyani, Revd Celia Apeagyei-Collins, Dr Tracy Cotterell, and Dr Al Barth – whose kindness, wisdom, sacrifice and encouragement have been a constant source of strength and inspiration. I cannot thank them enough.

I would also like to express my deep appreciation to the late Revd Dr Joel Edwards, Rt Revd Christopher Chessun, Dr Yoseph Mengestu, Andy Frost, John Tasker, Revd Margaret Evans, John Theuns and Dr John Jacob Woolf. Their advice, generosity and thoughtful challenges have been instrumental in shaping and refining this vision.

Finding a skilful and experienced editor is one thing, but finding an editor who not only possesses skill and experience but also truly believes in what you are writing is an even greater blessing. That is what Mary Davis has been to me. Thank you for stretching my thinking, making me work harder, and helping me articulate my thoughts more clearly. I am forever grateful.

Acknowledgements

To my family – your love is a daily reminder of God's goodness, teaching me to live in a posture of gratitude. Your support has been invaluable.

With all my heart, I dedicate this book to my dear sister in Christ, Clare Herriot – the most loving, kind and generous person I have ever known. Your dedication, creativity and tireless hard work have been instrumental in bringing the Gratitude Initiative to where it stands today. Thank you!

Introduction

It is amazing how an idea can come into our mind, find its way into our heart, consume our life and refuse to let go. Through time, that simple seed starts to germinate, unfolding and revealing itself. Its depth and content grow in us. Before it is fully ripe, we begin sharing its fruit out of pure excitement. Some people spit it out, saying that it tastes sour and bitter. We start to doubt our conviction of it.

However, despite the negative responses and self-doubt, the concept stubbornly remains. And then we understand where we went wrong. We served it before it was fully ripe. Finding people who believe in the potential of the unripe idea, against all odds, could be a matter of life and death.

This has been my journey with the concept of gratitude.

Having said that, the ultimate answer to the complex and multifaceted human predicament is unequivocally found in the gospel of Jesus Christ. There exists no other solution that comprehensively addresses the myriad questions posed by human existence and simultaneously facilitates the restoration of humanity to its Creator. Therefore, it is essential to understand that when we discuss the concept of gratitude in the context of this discussion, we are not introducing an alternative solution or an idea that diverts people from the central tenets of the gospel. In this book, gratitude is portrayed as a direct manifestation and practical outworking of the gospel. It is not a standalone concept but rather a posture that aligns with our created humanity.

This posture of gratitude empowers individuals to acknowledge and enjoy the Creator and his creation fully. Through gratitude, humans can acknowledge the primacy of the good, and this

Introduction

recognition allows them to enjoy a deeper connection with their Creator and the world around them. Gratitude, therefore, is not just a fleeting emotion but a profound and essential aspect of living a life that is aligned with the teachings of the gospel. Through the lens of gratitude, people either foster and cultivate (as disciples of Christ) or are prompted to sincerely seek a deeper, more meaningful relationship with both the divine and all of creation.

I wrote this book to take you through my own journey with gratitude and help you discover how it can transform your life. Chapter 1 sets the stage by exploring how my interest in gratitude began. In Chapter 2, we discuss why it is crucial for our polarised society to engage seriously with the concept of gratitude and recognise its importance in our collective life.

Chapter 3 offers a clear definition of the nature of gratitude and its benefits, setting the groundwork for understanding its role and significance. Chapter 4 addresses and clarifies several common misconceptions about gratitude, helping to refine our perspective.

In Chapter 5, we anchor gratitude in the biblical narratives and in theological thought, emphasising the importance of gratitude since creation and its significance in both social harmony and spiritual growth. Chapter 6 explores how gratitude acts as a dynamic force in social change and enhances our well-being by influencing and shaping our perspective. Chapter 7 concludes by highlighting the numerous benefits of cultivating a gratitude mindset, emphasising how this approach can positively impact our lives and society in the UK.

Throughout the book, you will find several 'In conversation' sections. These segments feature dialogues with researchers and thinkers who provide insights and reflections from their respective fields, enriching our understanding of gratitude.

In the appendices at the end of the book, you will find various ideas and resources on how to cultivate gratitude in daily life.

Introduction

Gratitude is a principle deeply valued and esteemed by modern society and the world's major religions. It is seen as something worthy of our attention and admiration. Even individuals who may not regularly practise gratitude themselves often recognise and appreciate its significance when they experience it being extended by others. Therefore, the principle of gratitude discussed in this book is universally applicable and will benefit readers from diverse backgrounds, regardless of their personal beliefs or practices. However, it is important to note that this book is informed and shaped by my Christian faith.

My journey as a Christian has profoundly influenced my understanding of gratitude, allowing me to reflect on it from various perspectives through the lens of the Scriptures. My faith has provided me with a unique framework to explore the multifaceted nature of gratitude, and I aim to share these insights with you throughout this book. As you read, you will discover that the teachings and stories within the Christian tradition have enriched my comprehension of gratitude, enabling me to appreciate its depth and significance in ways that might resonate with your own experiences. While the principles discussed are universally relevant, the Christian context in which they are presented offers additional layers of meaning and reflection. It is my hope that this exploration of gratitude, rooted in my Christian faith, will inspire and encourage you to cultivate a grateful heart, enriching your life and the lives of those around you.

1
My journey to this point

Around six o'clock in the evening I heard a knock at the front gate. Leaving what I was doing behind, I went to open the door. Three gentlemen were standing outside – two local police officers and one civilian. It was the civilian who spoke, asking me the whereabouts of my older brother. They had been told that there was an eighteen-year-old man at the address.

I knew who they were. I knew why they were there. They were looking for me.

Relaxed and calm as I could be, I told them that my brother was out and that he would not be back before 9.00 p.m. They said they would come back another time and left. Somehow, looking at my face, they thought I could not be the eighteen-year-old man they were looking for. Closing the door behind me, I breathed a long, slow sigh of relief and went to tell my mother what had happened. Panicking, she told me to grab a few clothes and we left the house in a hurry.

We took a taxi to the western side of Addis Ababa (then called Asmara Mengede) where my auntie used to live. We waited until dark before we went in, fearing that the neighbours would see us and inform the authorities. I stayed with her for about three months, never once leaving the house. During that time, the authorities repeatedly came to my mother's house asking for me, but she told them that she had no idea where I was.

At the time, Ethiopia was under a Communist regime and embroiled in a tense and protracted conflict with Eritrea. The government was recruiting and forcing young people to join the army to serve their country at the front lines. Two things concerned many young people at the time, besides their own personal circumstances: recruits were given short, inadequate training before being deployed to the front, and huge numbers of casualties flooded the local hospitals. The other pressing issue for many of us was the fact that we had many Eritrean friends and neighbours living with and alongside us. Going to war would mean fighting their brothers and sisters. That is, of course, the dilemma of a war of independence.

Resolved not to join the army, the only alternative for me (like many other young people at the time) was to leave Ethiopia and emigrate. Influenced by Hollywood, the USA became the preferred destination for most of us. To get to America, however, was impossible – unless you had a close relative who could send you an invitation and had the money to convince the embassy that you had a lot to lose in Ethiopia if you remained there.

I decided that Germany would be a good option – but getting a German visa was notoriously difficult. So, I planned to fly to Yugoslavia via Germany and stay in Germany instead of continuing to Yugoslavia. The next challenge was to get a passport, which was a lengthy and complicated process. Fortunately, we had a family friend who worked in a regional government office who provided letters of support, bypassing the local officials. Being in possession of a passport meant that checks by the airport officials would be minimal.

With ticket and passport in hand, I set off for the airport. My family was hopeful for my future, and they came to the airport to say goodbye. Leaving them and all that was familiar behind me, I passed through security and headed for the boarding gate, lining up for a final check of my ticket and passport.

The officer checking my documents asked me if I had a German transit visa. 'No, sir, I don't,' I replied. He explained how Germany had introduced new rules to stop people using this particular route to stay in the country. No one without a valid transit visa was allowed to board the plane. 'I am afraid you have to go to the German Embassy to get a transit visa and come back,' he said.

I froze, staring at him, expecting him somehow to change his mind. But he was adamant. I had to get a transit visa. I left the desk, found a chair and sat down, thinking how devastated my family would be. I didn't have any choice. I would have to face them and tell them the situation: there wasn't any other safe route I could now explore to leave the country. I had no option but to return home.

Two weeks later, a friend turned up at my house. He worked in the X-ray department at the Black Lion Hospital in Addis Ababa. Earlier that day, he'd met an English doctor who was on a short trip to Ethiopia to assist at the hospital. In the middle of their conversation, my friend asked her about the types of visa that the British Embassy issued. She said she had no idea but thought that they might give out tourist visas.

After work, my friend came round and insisted that I should go to the British Embassy to request a tourist visa. I laughed at him. 'Do you really expect, at a time like this, when so many young people are desperate to leave the country, that the British Embassy will give a tourist visa to a young man like me?' I refused to discuss it any further. For days, he kept on insisting. 'What do you have to lose? If you get the visa, that is great. If not, you will not be losing anything.'

Eventually and reluctantly, and to get him off my back, I decided to try. When I got to the embassy, I had to complete a form indicating the kind of visa I was applying for and pay the required amount. I was told to come back in two weeks' time for an interview. Only if they were satisfied with the interview would I be granted a visa.

During those two weeks, in preparation for the interview, I started reading up a bit about Britain for the first time, particularly about London and its tourist attractions. I went along for the interview with little hope of success. When I arrived at the embassy, a few people were queueing for the office where a gentleman behind a desk gave applicants their passports back. Some were asked to go down a corridor where they would find a receptionist directing them to an interview room.

When my turn came at the window, I handed the gentleman a document from my initial visit indicating that I had an interview. He looked through piles of passports, picked up mine and gave it to me. I stood there, waiting for him to give me further instructions. He looked back at me, wondering what was going on.

I opened the passport on a page where a receipt had been placed. And there was a visa. I kept standing there, thinking they must have made some kind of mistake. I'd just come for the interview.

The person behind me took the passport from me and said loudly, 'You have been given a visa to go to Great Britain within the next six months.'

I took my passport back and headed to the exit, expecting to be called back at any moment to be told that they had made a mistake. The journey from the main building to the gate was the longest journey ever.

A short time later, I landed at London Heathrow Airport. It was 3 September 1990.

Life in Britain

Fast forward nearly thirty years to May 2018.

I will never forget the encounter I had with an English couple in the West End of London late one Friday evening and how the power of gratitude was revealed to me in that conversation. As we were chatting, two people passed by, talking loudly and humorously about a political issue. We laughed at the conversation we'd overheard, but it developed into a serious discussion.

The lady started to tell me how ashamed she was of the state of her country, Britain. She started to list the causes of her shame:

My journey to this point

Brexit, the divisions in the country, hate crime, unjust immigration laws, racism. The list went on. From the way she looked at me – an African and someone who potentially could be affected by these issues – it was evident that she expected me to agree with her or add some more problems to the list. Instead, I said to her, 'I am sorry, madam. I don't agree with you.'

Surprised by my response, she asked me, 'What do you mean you don't agree with me?' I explained that, from my perspective, there are qualities in Great Britain which we sometimes take for granted. I listed a few of them which, in my opinion, deserved recognition, such as: generosity, equal rights, a pragmatic approach to life, a commitment to courteous coexistence, law-abiding citizenship, humane societal values, compassion and charity.

She could not believe that this African man had contradicted her and said, 'Forgive me for asking, but where are you from originally? How can you talk about Britain like this?'

I explained I was from Ethiopia and that I had come to Britain when Ethiopia was under Communist rule and in the midst of a war of independence. I had come as a young man, knowing nothing about Britain, not expecting to meet anyone at the airport and with only $250 in my pocket.

'From that first day,' I explained, 'I was received, given a place to live, money to live by, and an opportunity to work, to study and to be a contributor to society. I am what I am today by the grace of God and by the generosity of the British people. Therefore, when I talk about Britain, I cannot start with the negative – I begin by expressing my gratitude and celebrating the best that we have in Britain.'

At this point, the lady started crying. 'You have renewed my hope for my country,' she said. 'We are the ones who should be grateful for having migrants in our country. Where would Britain be without the migrant community?'

'No, we are the grateful ones,' I replied. 'No, we are,' she countered. And we continued reciprocating our gratitude! We chatted for a while, and the atmosphere created by our gratitude to each other was such that neither of us wanted it to end. Eventually we parted with a warm handshake. I am sure that if we had been in Africa, it would have been a hug!

As I reflected, I felt certain that if I'd had bad experiences in Britain and had wanted to share them with the woman, she would have listened to me without being defensive. Healing and reconciliation would no doubt have taken place. But I saw how gratitude catalysed and created the atmosphere necessary for a constructive conversation, leading to relational transformation.

My story matters as much as yours

I have had many similar conversations since then. I know that sharing my positive experience of Britain never fails to raise questions!

Am I saying that I haven't had any negative experiences in Britain as an immigrant?

Am I saying that Britain is a safe haven for all migrants?

Am I saying that I don't have anything to complain about?

The answer is no; I am not saying that. I have had negative experiences in Britain – sometimes directly related to the fact that I am an immigrant, sometimes because I am black. Moreover, working as a pastor for over eighteen years in a predominantly migrant church has given me an insight into the challenges, sufferings and negative experiences of people fleeing to Britain to escape persecution. Many people wait for years to hear about their fate from the Home Office.

I witnessed the impact of uncertainty and lack of permission to work and study experienced by people who have come to Britain seeking asylum. I've seen the economic, psychological and social impact of years of waiting. It is not my intention to deny those stories. As we have done as a Church for years, I believe

My journey to this point

in speaking truth to power and standing against corrupt and inhuman systems.

What I am saying is that the negative experiences should not be allowed to eradicate the positive ones. There are negative experiences and situations which should be addressed – but there are also positive experiences that should be acknowledged and celebrated.

As I've listened to people who have suffered as a consequence of migration laws in Britain, the thing that has surprised me is that they always either start or finish their story by mentioning someone who stood alongside them. Someone who supported them and became a voice for them from within the host nation. Sometimes their circumstances totally changed due to those individuals who chose to be a voice for the voiceless.

Therefore, in my view, it is appropriate to acknowledge the existence of both negative and positive stories and experiences. Talking exclusively about the negatives, as if there are no positives, quenches hope and appetite for change. It denies us access to people's imagination, where the source of the problems lies. Our interactions with and perceptions of others are shaped by our ideas, experiences and assumptions about them, which reside in our imagination. We only alter our views and interactions when we encounter information that contradicts our preconceived notions. By accessing human imagination, we create an environment or use an approach that encourages people to move beyond these ingrained misconceptions and prompts critical questioning.

Starting our conversations by appreciating the positive throws the negative into sharper focus and thus leads to change. It helps us to be objective, discussing the issue instead of the person.

In a multicultural society, every story matters. Each story has a right to be heard. If we reject the right of stories to be heard just because they are different from ours, we replicate the same behaviour that was imposed on us. We are perpetuating the very thing we are trying to see changed. Rather, we need to see the power of a collective, of how many different stories can be used as forces for good.

Gratitude is the overarching narrative that creates space for people with opposing stories to have constructive conversations, without having to give up their own convictions. Coming together around the banquet of gratitude means engaging in conversation which seeks a solution.

> 'Gratitude is the overarching narrative that creates space for people with opposing stories to have constructive conversations, without having to give up their own convictions.'

> 'Coming together around the banquet of gratitude means engaging in conversation which seeks a solution.'

Ideas do not arise in a vacuum. They come out of our observations, experiences and reflections. Let us walk alongside one another and explore whether gratitude can be a force for social transformation.

2

Why gratitude and why now?

I returned home, impressed by the relationship and harmony I had observed during the monthly meeting of church leaders from various backgrounds and ethnicities. The meeting had taken place at a Nigerian church in London, and the agenda for the day was a discussion on a week-long outreach event that was planned for their borough. The laughter, the hugging, the interaction, the attentiveness and the smiles between those leaders conveyed a message that all was well. The majority were Caucasians, but there were leaders from almost every continent. The prayer and singing were also collective, as if people had found a middle ground that didn't make others uncomfortable. The network had held similar events in previous years but, this year, the plans were scaled up, with a collective event at the end of the week. The leader coordinating the arrangements concluded the meeting by encouraging people to pray for the plan, to contribute towards the event as the Lord led them, and informing them that he would be looking for an auditorium that could hold 2,000 people.

I realised later that my first impressions were very superficial. They were shaped by surface-level interactions. It emerged that there were issues the leaders were not prepared to discuss. There was an enormous elephant in the room. Several of them, in fact.

The elephant in the room

The leader went on to announce that there was no auditorium available in the borough apart from the one where the current meeting was taking place. Naturally, the minister proposed that he was happy for the event to take place at his church. It could accommodate the expected numbers, and due to the centrality and capacity of the building, it was the ideal place for the planned event. But, for some reason, the coordinator insisted that there was no auditorium available. It didn't make sense.

People started to ask questions. If this building was available, why were they looking for another? The coordinator struggled to respond. At this point, a Caucasian Church of England priest stood up: 'If we use this building, some churches might not be willing to participate.'

'Is it because it is a Nigerian church?'

'Which churches wouldn't be willing to come here?'

'Tell us. We're all here.'

'Are you saying you are only comfortable when we are together behind closed doors?'

For the black, Asian and Latin American Christians in the meeting who had been with the group for many years, the announcement was a shock. People started to ask, 'Why wouldn't they want to come here? Are we not brothers and sisters in Christ? Are we not worshipping the same God?'

They could not understand why some churches among them would find it difficult to hold a public meeting in a building owned by one of them. They were also questioning which churches the Church of England minister was referring to, since almost all of the church leaders were present.

Nobody was able to give a satisfactory answer. Eventually, the heated discussion was interrupted by a white pastor who happened to be working in a Nigerian church. He explained that not everyone had the same level of understanding, and that this tendency to exclude was not just a problem for white Christians.

A few days later, I was privileged to talk with the chairman of the steering committee, Philip. He was very transparent and told me about the struggles they were having. He explained that, among the churches involved, some of the congregations had members from the diaspora and international community who were not yet ready to be inclusive in their practice. The churches with predominantly white congregations were comfortable interacting with ethnic minorities within their church buildings, but they found it difficult to show solidarity in a public domain. He also admitted that some of them were not prepared to put in adequate effort to see our differences as a strength and celebrate uniqueness as God's gift.

He explained how there were significant issues that needed to be openly addressed before biblical unity could materialise. They did not have a framework that could help raise those issues and pave the way for constructive conversations that would help them to move forward. Many of their leaders either didn't know how to do it or considered it too messy to handle.

If we wanted to see a collaborative mission front, it was clear that these issues – as well as many others – needed to be addressed. We wanted a mission where the diaspora, international and indigenous Christians were engaged together as a collective of believers reaching out to the diverse congregations, capturing the mission opportunity, and engaging in transforming the wider community. We had a long way to go.

A new framework

This story is not a rare occurrence. It is a common phenomenon in various relational contexts. Communication breakdown, longstanding animosity, resentment and suspicion are evident in many different parts of society – and they are major obstacles for collaborative mission and discipleship.

Gospel transformation must be evident not only in our relationship with God, but also with fellow human beings. Gospel mission is compelling, as the Lord said, when its uniting power is apparent in the community of believers: 'By this everyone will know that you are my disciples, if you love one another' (John 13:35).

In a broader sense, society is increasingly divided along social and political lines.

> 'It is finding and focusing on what people share in common – the common good – that sets the trajectory to the destination of understanding, reconciliation, harmony and justice.'

That is obvious, both in our most intimate relationships and in public policy debates. The divisions in politics, gender, sexuality, race, ethnicity, immigration, environmental protection and other areas are continuing to increase. In these contexts, it is finding and focusing on what people share in common – the common good – that sets the trajectory to the destination of understanding, reconciliation, harmony and justice. It does not mean that in the pursuit of social harmony we sacrifice justice or truth, or that we accommodate ideas which are contrary to our beliefs. It means we start our conversation by affirming and recognising our common humanity.

> 'We start our conversation by affirming and recognising our common humanity.'

My engagement in multicultural conversations over the years has convinced me of the need for a new framework to help us talk about difficult issues in a constructive way. My discussion with Philip – and particularly his reference to a lack of framework – stayed with me for a long time. That experience opened my eyes to see that it is a common phenomenon. People told me that they had tried to raise those difficult issues previously and, in the process, either got hurt or found that the emotion behind the issues frustrated the conversation. They felt that they had explored every avenue. They knew where each one led. So why start the journey?

Nobody denied the importance of raising issues and listening to each other's stories. However, the complexity of the issues, the historical baggage associated with them, and unsuccessful past conversations created fatigue. Successfully addressing difficult issues would only be possible when people found a safe environment, where there was relational capital and they felt free to make mistakes. In a safe environment, people feel free to be vulnerable, are willing to be challenged, and are open to listening and understanding the story and experience of the other. However, such an environment is rare.

> 'In a safe environment, people feel free to be vulnerable, are willing to be challenged, and are open to listening and understanding the story and experience of the other.'

Going deeper into gratitude

As I prayed, observed and reflected on my interactions with others, on the successful and unsuccessful exchanges, why I succeeded in one and not the other, I began to observe a pattern.

I realised that when I started my conversation with my positive experiences and observations, people felt at ease and were attentive to the negative issues I raised later. However, when I started my conversation with the negative – sometimes in response to a direct question from them – the relationship stayed stagnant and the conversation rarely progressed positively.

> 'When I started my conversation with my positive experiences and observations, people felt at ease and were attentive to the negative issues I raised later.'

I observed the negative narratives that dominated the public arena – the single story defining the way we see and relate to others. I saw 'the danger of a single story' that author Chimamanda Ngozi Adiche eloquently describes.[1] I began to see the need for

Why gratitude and why now?

balance and a different approach to tackle our society's social ills. The stories about the migrant community and the host nation, the loud negative noise of the minority disabling the majority's positive voice, feeding and creating all kinds of extremism in all camps. This needed to change. Even in the Church, we observe and interact with the debates in the public arena but often shy away from openly tackling controversial issues. This can leave us vulnerable to similar divisions in our own Christian communities.

My own experience of Christian grace and of generosity also played its part. Growing up in a religious family, my 'sin' was constantly highlighted to me, making me feel condemned. It created an enormous burden within me that whatever I did had to be right before God. This pressure didn't ever help, because I always fell short of God's requirements, no matter how hard I tried. I was not learning how to motivate myself – I was simply responding to external pressure. Eventually, I was so tired that I gave up and began living a selfish lifestyle that I knew wouldn't meet with God's approval.

However, it was experiences of grace in my life – of God's movement towards me in love while I was still a sinner – that shocked, changed and motivated me to begin really living for him. Any and all positive change that has happened in my life occurred via the experience of his grace.

Now, if I needed grace to change my thoughts and course of action, then why should I expect others to change without it? I realised that there cannot be true repentance in the presence of condemnation. Communicating grace rather than condemnation gives each of us the ability to awaken people's imagination. It helps them to consider and, with the help of Christ, overcome their own sin, creating an inner momentum for change. If people are in survival mode, made to feel threatened or uncomfortable by a conversation, they won't be able to take in any new information, let alone allow it to challenge them and transform any pre-existing wrong conclusions or assumptions. But when we create an environment where people feel at ease, they get a chance to just listen and perhaps allow their thinking to be challenged. It is in this atmosphere of grace that an internal drive for positive change can begin.

I believe gratitude is a vehicle that communicates grace to others.

I believed this so strongly that I did a doctoral level study on it. I undertook research to examine the current state of relations between the diaspora (or international community) and native British Christian leaders in London.[2] This lengthy study confirmed my convictions. Participants were selected from leadership positions of various ethnicities, denominations and para-church organisations. They had different spheres of influence and positions in their respective organisations, and included both men and women. All thirty leaders, who were from different geographical locations in London, participated in completing questionnaires, and I invited seven of those leaders to participate in a focus group. Additionally, three bishops and three para-church ministry directors, all of whom had London-wide responsibility, participated in semi-structured one-to-one interviews.

> 'I believe gratitude is a vehicle that communicates grace to others.'

The first list of questions presented to the selected leaders included questions that dealt only with the state of the relationship between the two groups of community leaders. Participants were not aware of the follow-up questions about gratitude. The results were astounding. The problems they identified as barriers between the two groups of community leaders correlated directly with descriptions associated with the benefits of gratitude.

> 'The problems they identified as barriers between the two groups correlated directly with descriptions associated with gratitude.'

Why gratitude and why now?

Problems	Gratitude
Lack of communication	Makes honest communication possible
Undermining others	Highlights the worthiness of others
Ignoring the gifts of others	Recognises the gifts and contributions of others
Suspicion	Negates mutual suspicion and builds trust
Lack of openness	Breaks barriers
Prejudice	Brings down prejudice
Failure to accommodate differences	Helps us see others as Christ sees them
Superiority	Changes our outlook on others

The correlation between identified problems and gratitude

Gratitude, defined as an acknowledgement of the good, is a catalyst that creates the atmosphere necessary for constructive conversation, leading to improved listening to, and understanding of, people 'other' than us. In addition, it creates a space where people can voluntarily confront any wrongheaded internal images of others without coming under external pressure to do so. This avoids people going into survival mode – 'fight or flight' – and shutting the conversation down.

Gratitude helps us to listen to each other's opinions. We won't get anyone to agree with us if no one will listen to us in the

> 'Gratitude helps us to listen to each other's opinions.'

first place. It is not political correctness we need – it is emotional correctness in order to win the attention of others, even those who don't agree with our opinions. Gratitude helps us to be emotionally correct when we engage with people who are different from us, because it focuses us on them and their strengths rather than ourselves. We can move from being closed off and defensive to being open and appreciative of what they bring to the conversation.

The need to access the social imagination

'Social imagination' is a term used in the field of sociology to describe a framework for understanding the social reality that places personal experiences within a broader social and historical context. Our social imagination is carved through time and informed by our experience, cultural consumption and history. As such, the 'carving' process happens within the society in which we live.

As individuals we each have a unique imagination, of course, but social imagination plays a significant part in our relatedness – in other words, our social connections, relationships and interactions.

Different forces dictate and shape our individual imaginations as members of a society – some are historical, while others stem from our current thoughts, experiences and ideologies. In order to see a change in our social relationships, we need to see a change in our social imagination.

Exploring how our social imagination might have contributed to current social problems is an enormous but essential task. At the same time, identifying a conceptual framework which is effective and validated across academic disciplines is essential for altering how members of society view themselves and each other. Such a framework could enable individual and therefore societal transformation.

In the increasingly multicultural society of

> 'Identifying a conceptual framework which is effective and validated across academic disciplines is essential for altering how members of society view themselves and each other.'

Britain – with its many stories, experiences and perspectives – the concept needs to provide commonality. It must resonate with individuals; it must communicate how it could serve and empower them and show the way forward in building personal and social well-being.

What could help us challenge and change our preconceived ideas and images of others, by creating room for us to encounter our prejudice?

What could encourage a strength-oriented approach to community development, considering the positive contributions from our neighbours and the thousands who serve our communities every day?

What could create the atmosphere necessary to make constructive conversation possible?

What could embolden us to fight for justice and, at the same time, achieve the relational transformation that would address the causes of the injustice?

What could help us win the war rather than dwell on the battle? What could help us eradicate the sources and causes of injustice rather than just getting justice?

What could help us to build bridges between communities to make cross-cultural mission possible?

What could help us prepare the way for the Lord?

The need for a free psychological space

I believe a new approach is needed. I am advocating for an approach which creates a 'free psychological space' where people can encounter their erroneous imaginations and perceive the experience and personhood of the other, a space which enables them to be free to listen attentively.

Psychological space in this context is to do with the state of our mind in dealing with external – as well as internal – facts and influences. There are external situations, challenges and threats that could invade our psychological space and keep us busy in responding to them. When our mind is busy responding to challenges and possible threats, it loses its ability to listen, focus or take inventory on itself. If we are to encourage self-reflection and enhance our ability to listen and achieve a change of mindset, we need free psychological space – in other words, a space that allows us to process thoughts, emotions and experiences without overwhelm or distraction.

> 'We need a space that allows us to process thoughts, emotions and experiences without overwhelm or distraction.'

The conceptual framework or approach that would allow society to address its problems – its divisions and disunities – needs to fulfil certain criteria.

- It must uphold the cause and struggle for justice.
- It must create the relational transformation that could significantly dent the causes of injustice.
- It must catalyse new beginnings for a better future.
- It must create a platform where we can remember the past together (because remembering and recognising past injustices demonstrates a commitment to showing love to the wrongdoer and overcoming evil with good and is an essential leg of the journey towards building a just society).
- It must be a metanarrative big enough to accommodate opposing views and create an environment where constructive conversation occurs.
- It must help us to speak the truth in love – a tricky balance to hold when emotions run high.

> 'The framework should help us to speak the truth in love, a balance that is tricky to hold when emotions are high.'

Why gratitude and why now?

The concept that fulfils all those criteria and creates the psychological space necessary to change the social imagination is gratitude. Gratitude does not turn a blind eye to injustice or negative realities. It does not substitute a 'rosy' or 'romantic' picture for concrete facts. It accepts these realities for what they are, but intentionally starts the conversation by acknowledging and focusing on the good, bringing positive vitality to conversations about change.

Psychological space is crucial for the introduction of a new perspective – a space free from noise, from a fight to defend oneself or to protect one's opinion; a space free from the presence of fear or condemnation. A psychological space where someone needs to defend themselves, feels threatened or condemned, and is therefore forced to hide their true feelings and opinions, cannot be productive. In a crowded psychological space like this, new perspectives fail to develop and wrong imaginations remain unchallenged. Consequently, conversations remain superficial and do not progress.

It follows, then, that a genuine encounter happens in the context of a free psychological space – a space where someone feels present, not as if they are standing before a judge to be interrogated and criticised, but rather as if they are welcomed as a fellow human being, with both weaknesses and strengths. In such a space, the strengths and the willingness to engage are recognised, acknowledged and celebrated. Here, individuals are free from the need to fight, defend or hide. They are unburdened and open to listening. As a result, two kinds of encounter occur: one with our own opinions, actions, prejudices, misconceptions, biases or wrong imaginations; and another with the other person's stories, experiences and personhood. Both of these encounters will foster the transformation that leads to healthier relationships.

How Jesus created a psychological space for Zacchaeus

Jesus' transformative approach to sinners changed lives and restored relationships. The Gospels are full of examples showing how he signalled his love and acceptance of them, irrespective of the wrongs they had committed.[3] This acceptance created a free psychological space, free from condemnation, enabling individuals to confront their sin and commit to making amends where they could.

His profound love was never an endorsement of wrongdoing. He never accepted their sin or the wrongs they had committed lightly – far from it. But he knew that undeserving love was what led people to encounter their sin and change their course of action. His grace motivated people to acknowledge their faults and alter their paths.

That is what we see in the story of Zacchaeus in Luke 19:1-10. As a collector of taxes, Zacchaeus was a capitalist and a crook, a notorious person who committed injustice, someone who collaborated with the oppressors. His actions were well known to those around him. Everyone knew who he was and what he did. And he knew what everyone said and thought about him. But he was benefiting from the system, so he continued in his practice unrepentantly until he met Jesus, who risked being misunderstood by others in order to associate with him.

The people all talked about Zacchaeus as 'a sinner', but Jesus' opinion and focus couldn't have been more different. When he talked about Zacchaeus, he said that 'this man, too, is a son of Abraham' (verse 9). It wasn't Zacchaeus's behaviour, sin and injustice that occupied Jesus' attention. When he started talking to him, that wasn't the focus of their conversation. That wasn't what dictated the terms of Jesus' relationship with him.

Jesus approached Zacchaeus by focusing on and celebrating his humanity – the fact that Zacchaeus was created in the image of God and a descendant of Abraham. Jesus didn't say anything about

Why gratitude and why now?

Zacchaeus's wrong practice. Instead, he created a psychological space where Zacchaeus could encounter his sin himself. There is something about approaching a relationship based on someone's strengths – even while there are weaknesses to talk about – that is powerful enough to expose a person's heart to themselves.

Before his encounter with Jesus, Zacchaeus's mind was busy defending and justifying his actions to himself and others. Meeting Jesus, Zacchaeus experienced a non-judgemental relationship with him where his strengths (his humanity and connection with Abraham) were the focus. In that approach, Zacchaeus found a free psychological space where he saw and encountered, for the first time, the injustice and ugliness of his actions. He was quick to respond. His perspective of life and values had been radically changed and he not only repented, but he immediately proposed to return four times what he had taken.

In some respects, we all experience salvation in a similar way. Jesus embraces us while we are his enemies, without any preconditions. It is his embrace that reassures us, but also reveals our sin to us and leads us to repentance. There cannot be true repentance in the presence of condemnation and a crowded psychological space. Condemnation doesn't communicate hope for restoration of the broken relationship. Even if I repent, there is no guarantee that the relationship will be amended. Condemnation doesn't communicate love, but judgement, and that triggers a tendency to self-defence. Anticipating judgement, reasoning and seeking to defend ourselves, our minds will be crowded. We will lack the capacity to see things from others' point of view, or to see our own fault.

Gratitude is a catalyst for creating the environment necessary for new beginnings and better futures. As much as it is vital to hear negative experiences and injustices in

> 'Gratitude is a catalyst for creating the environment necessary for new beginnings and better futures.'

order to understand and address them, it is also essential to create a platform where positive stories can be heard. It is positive experiences that will create the energy for change and help paint a picture of how a desired outcome might look.

Using exposition as a metaphor

In the Christian tradition, expository preaching is the art of explaining and applying the meaning and intent of a biblical text. Pastor and author Alistair Begg defines expository preaching as, 'Unfolding the text of Scripture in such a way that it makes contact with the listener's world while exalting Christ and confronting them with the need for action.'[4]

The goal of exposition is not only to shed light on a portion of Scripture – or, to use the technical term, exegete the text. If that is all that happens, the work is only half done. There is a second goal of exposition: to apply the text to the context of the listeners so that they may be able to make it their own and respond accordingly, allowing the word of God to transform their lives. Since transformation is always the end goal of exposition, it cannot only be an exercise of the mind. The heart must also be involved.

The necessary involvement of the heart compels a preacher to make room to empathise with the perspectives, situations, struggles and challenges of their listeners. In the process of working out, under God, how to apply the text, the preacher will discover wrongs which need to be corrected alongside good that needs to be affirmed. Similarly, we can see that a posture of gratitude, starting with affirming the good, can be instrumental in opening the hearts of listeners. It gives them both the hope and the courage needed for change.

Paul in Ephesians 5:13 speaks in a similar manner. 'But everything exposed by the light becomes visible – and everything that is illuminated becomes a light.' This is a process that has transformation as its end goal. At first, the light shines onto a person, exposing the 'darkness' of a wrong ideology, for example. However, this is just the first stage of the process. For someone to appreciate the true nature of their actions and then change, they must be illuminated from within. There is value in someone pointing out an error to them, but change will only really come when they are able to see the error for themselves. Once they have made a choice to change, the darkness has gone. They have been illuminated by the truth and have themselves become a light. Another light to push back the darkness.

Our approach, then, is what allows a person to let this light enter into their being. Instead of feeling threatened, they are met with empathy. Instead of facing condemnation and humiliation, the good is acknowledged. Instead of the mind shifting into survival mode and defensive actions, it relaxes, creating the vulnerability needed to address the wrongs in their lives and relationships.

Only exposing someone's wrongdoings, negative thoughts or ideology might lead the perpetrator to condemnation – but it will not lead to transformation. If we are satisfied with the discomfort our condemnation brings to the life of the individual, then there's no need for an alternative approach. However, if we want to see transformation take place, our approach should always include empathy and affirmation of the good.

> 'Only exposing someone's wrongdoings, negative thoughts or ideology might lead the perpetrator to condemnation – but it will not lead to transformation.'

That empathy comes from a deeper understanding of the condition of humanity, the commonality of our fallenness and the humility to consider the fact that we might have done the same thing had we been in similar circumstances. It is also the understanding that there is good in the life of the perpetrator before us. If we don't believe that there is any good within them, then the very exercise of exposing their wrongs is in vain. Rather, as Martin Luther King Jr articulated, we should remember that 'within the best of us, there is some evil, and within the worst of us, there is some good'.[5] Gratitude requires us to embrace these truths and aim for transformation by tackling the wrongs from a place of affirmation rather than condemnation.

It is clear that the aim of biblical exposition extends beyond just exegeting the text. Done properly, it also involves applying its wisdom to the listeners' context. We have seen how this dual process facilitates personal ownership and encourages a transformative response. If transformation is the ultimate goal, then exposition necessitates engagement of not only the mind but the heart. It is only in connecting the truth of the text with someone's perspective, struggles and challenges that openness to receiving correction and exhortations can begin in earnest.

Likewise, gratitude – rooted in an acknowledgement of the good – serves as a wise starting point, fostering openness, hope and courage for change. As I saw the nature and depth of gratitude unfold in my life through the years, as I shared with others, read about it and used it in my conversations, I came to realise that gratitude can enable powerful transformation – not only of individuals but of societies.

> 'Gratitude can enable powerful transformation – not only of individuals but of societies.'

The hurdle

Western leaders attempting to tackle division, whether within the Christian community or within wider society, have tended to emphasise exposing error. They expect individuals to shoulder personal and collective responsibility for these errors, usually through a call to acknowledge and repent of past wrongs, including any involvement of institutions to which they belong.

The call for repentance usually comes from the victims of injustice or wrongs. In the Western context, this particularly comes from ethnic minority communities. In the Church, many services have taken place where the confession of past wrongs has been made and forgiveness requested. These occasions of repentance do have spiritual and societal value on their own and are a step in the right direction. They have even, at times, succeeded in changing practices. But they ultimately fail to bring about the desired result – the transformation of relationships between communities. Continuous failure of this approach has created exhaustion and scepticism around further sincere endeavours to bring communities together, compounding resentment and creating a unity that is superficial and fragile.

There are several reasons why the desired result has not materialised. To begin with, the call to repentance from ethnic minorities has been concerned with not only the past wrongs but also the present relational problems. Implicitly, what the ethnic minorities have been asking is, 'You are treating us and relating to us in the same way you treated us before, so please change.' They are asking for a transformed relationship. However, at least two criteria must be fulfilled for true repentance to happen. First, the people or community called to repentance have to encounter, in the true sense of the word, the magnitude of the wrongs committed; and second, they must be willing to take personal or communal responsibility for what happened.

But these two criteria are not fulfilled, because of unanswered questions in the minds of those called to repentance, such as, 'Those were the actions of our grandparents, over which we had no control at all, so why should we apologise and repent now?' In many cases, people need to be helped to see that, although they were not primary actors in the injustices of the past, they are very often contemporary beneficiaries of the action, either in obvious ways (such as Britain still benefiting from cheap imports from former colonies), or in more indirect ways (such as an inherited psychology of white supremacy and the need to repent for current failure to take any action to redress continuing injustices).[6]

People could have historical knowledge of the wrongs done and despise them, but at the same time genuinely fail to comprehend the detrimental consequences for the descendants of the people affected. Additionally, they may not recognise their own position as beneficiaries of such wrongs. The tone of the call for repentance has failed to appreciate this fact and, at times, it has tended to be condemnatory. It is human nature to be defensive when condemned and so give lip service to avoid unnecessary confrontation. As mentioned before, there cannot be true repentance in the presence of condemnation. Condemnation does not communicate hope for change, nor does it promise acceptance if repentance occurs. As we saw, it is Jesus' unconditional love towards sinners, his death for us 'while we were sinners' (Romans 5:8), which exposes sin, causes people to repent and motivates believers to change their way of life.

Resentment, if allowed, can deter the reconciliation process and cause the oppressed to become what they hate in others. In his novel *Cry, the Beloved Country*, Alan Paton narrates the detrimental effect of apartheid for the black South Africans. In the middle of the narrative, he includes a surprising statement made by a black priest to his friend, expressing his fear of hatred and resentment: 'I have one great fear in my heart, that one day when they are turned to loving, they will find that we are turned to hating.'[7]

Resentment tints people's perception of reality and causes them to propagate a single story against the other, ignoring positive contributions and good stories. Pursuing this path not only keeps people in the past (at the cost of their own future), perpetuating anger and hatred, but it also makes them vulnerable to extremists who may use them to promote their views and lead to even deeper

Why gratitude and why now?

division. Creating a non-threatening space where the perpetrator can encounter the wrongs done and identify with the pains caused is a prerequisite for true repentance, a beginning for the healing process and the transformation of our communal relationships.

Community transformation has to do with altering the nature of relatedness and changing the nature of the conversation. In this regard, author Peter Block, founder of the Common Good Alliance, expounds the role of language in the community transformation process. He refers to author and lecturer Werner Erhard's conviction that no transformation is possible without change in the conversation. As the context informs language and moulds action, language also changes the way people perceive their context and relate to it.[8] By language, he means not only speech, but also those things that shape and inform discourse, such as imagination, perception and the art of listening. If what people *say* about others changes, then their actions and attitude towards others will also change. This is in line with biblical teaching. In the book of James the tongue is described as an influential part of our body, likened to the rudder of a ship or a forest fire (James 3:1–12). How we speak can have a profound effect on our actions, shaping our destiny.

The question is not whether the Church needs intercultural and inter-racial dialogue in our society today. Instead, we should be discussing what kind of pragmatic approach addresses the interests and struggles of those involved and how believers can engage with it. Past strategies have often fallen short in creating an environment conducive to authentic conversation. This has led to superficial responses and impeded long-lasting relational change.

A fresh approach is essential, one that promotes active listening and open dialogue, one that allows room for people to make appropriate responses. The need is for a framework that proposes steps for the process of building unity and collaboration which leads to mission and community transformation.

Why gratitude and why now?

It is the premise of this book that expressing gratitude (whether by simply celebrating the common good or recognising another's specific contribution and enriching presence) creates that framework. Expressing gratitude:

- creates a context where people can:
  - raise issues without condemning and isolating others
  - hear people's stories in a spirit of openness and
  - constructively discuss problems in order to achieve harmony;
- builds bridges for multicultural and collaborative mission;
- makes people happier at an individual level;
- motivates the recipients of appreciation, as well as the rest of the community, to make a greater contribution to wider society;
- encourages community cohesion and promotes societal harmony, as people actively contribute to the common good;
- offers an alternative positive outlook of being thankful where, in the words of a common idiom, the glass is seen as half full rather than half empty;
- fosters a new and positive way of relating both to ourselves individually and to one another corporately.

The growing interest in gratitude in the disciplines of sociology and psychology, with the longstanding teaching and wisdom of the Bible, underscores the important role gratitude will play in the future of our society. However, it will not be without its challenges.

Our present Western culture does not acknowledge the giftedness of life. A stranger is seen as a potential enemy. Individualism – or the premise of standing on our own two feet, not needing anyone else – is considered an accomplishment. This kind of social climate fails to generate the relational good which is characteristic of friendship or civility. In this context, a posture of gratitude, taking a moment to reflect – on what has been achieved, the resources at our disposal and the people involved to make it happen – will have a far-reaching individual, social and spiritual impact. Gratitude inspires us to allow the giftedness of our total existence to shape the way we view the world.

Drawing from biblical, theological, psychological and social perspectives, a comprehensive understanding of gratitude encompasses the following:

- Gratitude is an attitude that acknowledges the giftedness of life.
- It recognises the image of God in others.
- It appreciates the interdependency of human life.
- It acknowledges that life is richer and improved because of the presence of the other.
- It is a determination to imitate Christ, who chose to see a person's value, despite all their weaknesses and in spite of the evil in them.
- It involves the practice of accepting and acknowledging the other in the same way that Christ accepts and recognises us.
- As a reflection of Philippians 4:8 ('whatever is true, whatever is noble, whatever is right, whatever is pure, whatever is lovely, whatever is admirable – if anything is excellent or praiseworthy'), gratitude has a role for moral development.
- It embodies the wisdom of God, communicating hope for renewed relationships.
- It acts as a catalyst for creating space for new beginnings.
- It demonstrates a belief that there is good in others.
- It is a universally admired concept, across cultures and backgrounds.
- It is gentle and disarming, and encourages reciprocity.
- It is a remedy for insatiable yearnings and the ills of life.

3
Gratitude explored

Both of us were in the midst of a journey across the vast expanse of the United States. Initially separated on the first leg of our journey, fate – or perhaps God – brought us together for the subsequent connecting flight. As our aircraft ascended into the sky, Derick delved into his work, immersing himself in a document with rows of numbers. Meanwhile, I attempted to lose myself in a book. I didn't anticipate any interaction between us. However, approximately twenty minutes into our flight, Derick completed his task and, with a deep breath, initiated conversation: 'Are you interested in numbers?' he asked. My response was noncommittal: 'Not particularly. Why do you ask?' Derick told me about his profession as an accountant, expressing a fondness for numbers, particularly when they harmonise seamlessly.

Thus began a profound exchange. After acquainting me with his occupation and how long he had been working in it, Derick turned his attention to me, prompting inquiries about my own work and leading to a series of discussions surrounding my ministry. Our conversation meandered through various topics – the gospel, church dynamics, the concept of gratitude. Eventually, a contemplative silence enveloped Derick before he embarked on a poignant narrative about gratitude, intertwined with reflections on his upbringing.

He began with an ode to the transformative influence of teachers in the lives of their students. He recounted his humble beginnings, hailing from a modest family as the middle child among three boys. Born into a lineage of hardworking farmers, his father, captivated by a deep-seated affection for his vocation, harboured reservations about the pursuit of education for his children. Education was not esteemed within their familial tradition, and thus, his father discouraged his sons from pursuing academic endeavours, preferring instead to regale them with tales of their agricultural heritage.

Despite his father's aversion to formal education, governmental mandates compelled Derick to attend school until a prescribed grade level. Initially resistant, his defiance manifested in disruptive behaviour within the classroom, earning him a reputation as a troubled student. His aspirations did not extend beyond joining his father in the family business, and he relished the weekends spent working alongside him on the farm.

But the trajectory of his life took an unforeseen turn in fifth grade upon encountering Mr Solomon, a mathematics teacher whose approach differed markedly from that of his previous maths teacher, as well as the other teachers he had. While other educators admonished him for his disruptions, Mr Solomon displayed unwavering patience and a genuine interest in Derick's life outside the classroom. Their interactions, characterised by empathy and personalised attention, fostered a sense of validation and worth within Derick. Despite his unruly behaviour, Mr Solomon saw beyond the facade of defiance, recognising latent potential waiting to be nurtured. Gradually, Derick underwent a transformation, fuelled by Mr Solomon's unwavering belief in his capabilities. Encouraged by his teacher's affirmation, Derick began to apply himself diligently to his studies, achieving remarkable academic success. Mr Solomon's consistent encouragement and recognition of his achievements served as a beacon of hope amid the prevailing cynicism of his other instructors.

Eventually becoming a successful chartered accountant, Derick attributed his accomplishments to the mentorship and guidance of Mr Solomon, whose unwavering belief in his potential catalysed a profound metamorphosis in his life. He didn't ignore the bad behaviours but decided to tackle them by giving priority to acknowledging and celebrating the good in Derick. The approach of the other teachers had been the reverse. Derick explained how their style reinforced his bad behaviour, as it didn't give him any hope for change or help him to recognise his potential. Reflecting on his journey, Derick recognised that Mr Solomon had chosen the gratitude approach, which prioritised acknowledgement and celebration of his virtues over condemnation of his flaws, offering him a pathway to self-discovery and success.

He turned to me and concluded: 'All this is to say that I get it. The gratitude approach works.'

The benefits of gratitude

Several psychologists have grappled with the task of defining gratitude, a concept that proves to be elusive and multifaceted. Even esteemed figures in the field, such as Dr Robert Emmons, who has significantly advanced our understanding of gratitude in contemporary times, have acknowledged the challenge.[1] Emmons characterises gratitude as 'a multi-layered concept that defies easy description or analysis', highlighting the complexity inherent in its definition.[2]

Across the disciplines of psychology and sociology, gratitude is approached, examined and defined primarily through its perceived benefits. Scholars explore the question of how gratitude enhances and enriches the psychological and relational well-being of both individuals and society, using this starting point to discover its essence. Increasingly, scholars across these diverse fields agree on the overarching notion that gratitude exerts positive influences across all dimensions of human life, underlining its universal significance and impact.

> 'Across the disciplines, gratitude is approached, examined and defined primarily through its perceived benefits.'

Gratitude explored

In the wide realm of psychology, gratitude emerges as a profound acknowledgement of the benefits bestowed upon an individual, where the origin of such benefits lies external to the self.[3] Gratitude is thus appreciating the good things that come from outside sources. These benefits go beyond mere material things and include emotional and spiritual dimensions. The display of gratitude resonates not only in the attitude towards the benefactor and the gift, but also in the effusion of positive emotions experienced by the recipient.[4] Central to this display of attitude and emotional experience is the concept of unmerited merit – an acknowledgement of the unearned additions of value woven into a person's existence.

Examining the state of emotions, Robert Solomon, in his seminal work *The Passions*, defines gratitude as inherently self-esteeming, settled within the complex tapestry of positive and negative passions that define the human quest for existential meaning.[5] To put it another way, gratitude boosts our self-esteem and fits into the mix of good and bad feelings that shape our search for meaning. However, gratitude transcends mere emotional expression; it emerges as a virtue, a moral compass guiding individuals towards a profound appreciation for life's manifold blessings. While emotions can be fleeting, seeing gratitude as a core value means making a dedicated effort to embed it in our everyday routines and behaviours. Gratitude propels individuals towards proactive engagement with life, encouraging an innate inclination to discern and celebrate the positives amid the complexities of existence.

> 'Gratitude propels individuals towards proactive engagement with life.'

Yet, with the exaltation of gratitude, psychologists issue a note of caution, aware that indiscriminate application of gratitude can lead to complacency or to the enabling of detrimental circumstances. For example, being grateful for a toxic job or abusive relationship could discourage necessary action, lead people to invalidate their own feelings of anger, fear or sadness, and unintentionally reward abusive behaviours, thus reinforcing the dynamics. Many psychologists assert that true gratitude necessitates discernment – a perceptive understanding of the situational context and a genuine appreciation for the benefactor's contribution.[6] Thus, gratitude alternates between a fleeting emotional response and a deep-seated part of one's ethical and moral framework. As it does so, it beckons individuals to navigate the maze of human experience with humility, discernment and profound appreciation.[7]

Moreover, gratitude is not seen as just a personal trait; it also has profound social and relational effects. Sociologists view gratitude as a positive catalyst for social relations. They affirm that grateful individuals are more likely to exhibit compassion and altruism, leading to stronger social bonds and reciprocity. Studies have shown that expressing gratitude can even influence others to behave more altruistically.[8] In essence, gratitude serves as a moral compass, guiding individuals towards prosocial behaviour and reinforcing positive relationships. Its potential extends beyond personal well-being to bridging divides and fostering reconciliation in communities. As such, gratitude is understood in sociology as holding the promise of creating a more empathetic and interconnected society.

> 'Sociologists view gratitude as a positive catalyst for social relations.'

The nature of gratitude

Theologians take a different approach. Rather than starting their discussions of gratitude with its benefits, theology begins with the nature of gratitude. Gratitude, in theological terms, is acknowledging and responding to the goodness of God manifested in his person and his creation. It is a proactive engagement with acknowledging the good, making it a primary orientation in life. As such, gratitude in theology is the natural response of creation to the Creator. It is also the posture that enables created beings to connect with their Creator and navigate through life.[9]

Gratitude is *not* something extra that is added to life by practising a positive way of thinking. It is more foundational and intrinsic to our being. It is something that practising a more positive way of thinking might help unearth. A posture of gratitude is, therefore, a natural and beneficial stance in life for both human and environmental flourishing, one that brings glory to God. The Bible suggests that negative emotions in the human heart (greed, prejudice and so on) are consequences of what theologians call 'the Fall' of humanity. Gratitude is seen in Scripture to be a pre-Fall inner disposition that enabled humans to enjoy the gift of creation as well as its giver.[10] If we observe the pattern of the Fall in Genesis, we can see that it is when questioning the goodness of the Creator that humans abandoned their natural posture of gratitude. This ultimately led to the rebellion of humanity against God, with the emergence of negative emotions and the tendency to focus primarily on the wrong in situations and in other people.

Gratitude does not fluctuate according to external circumstances or situations. Instead, it is a stable internal trait or quality. It doesn't start from our external situations – they don't determine when is or isn't the right or wrong time or situation to be grateful. It is a theologically informed recognition and inner commitment to live life by prioritising the acknowledgement of the good. Recognising the theological insights which legitimise and encourage an attitude of gratitude provides a strong foundation for practising gratitude in every situation. They help to remind us that gratitude is founded on the truth about the Creator and us as his creation. In opposition to this encouragement, the messages and experiences of evil set out to destroy or make us doubt these truths. Evil will always try to deny the fact that we are more than our negative experiences.

Gratitude explored

Another way to look at it is that gratitude resembles love. The way love engages with evil will be different from the way hate engages with evil. We understand from the Bible that God is love. The greatest commandment (understood as the fulfilment of all commandments) is loving God with all our heart and loving our neighbours as we love ourselves.[11] This means we are commanded to function from a place of love. Not because there is no evil in the world or nothing to hate, but because we hate evil from the inner posture of love. Just because there is evil to hate, we don't let hate become our inner posture. The inner posture of love empowers and teaches us how to hate rightly – and for the right reason. Psalm 97:10 tells us: 'Let those who love the LORD hate evil.' Therefore, we love before we hate. We function from a place of love. Love teaches us what to hate, because when we truly love what is good, we must also reject what harms or opposes it.

Paul's explanation of love in his first letter to the Corinthian church lines up with what we are saying here. 'Love does not delight in evil but rejoices with the truth' (1 Corinthians 13:6).

In the theological definition of gratitude, there is no excess gratitude as there is nothing called excess love. If we function from love, we shouldn't put a caveat on love, questioning what love's response to evil should be. If we truly love, we will know when to hate. If our stance in life is gratitude, we shouldn't worry about how to respond to evil or even how to exercise gratitude in the presence of wrong. Even in abusive situations, adopting a grateful posture can help the abused not to be defined by their negative experiences.[12] This doesn't mean that abuse is ignored or tolerated. Instead, it enhances the healing process and empowers the victim to take the appropriate action to bring justice. Gratitude

> 'In the theological definition of gratitude, there is no excess gratitude as there is nothing called excess love.'

doesn't shy away from confronting evil but starts from a different place – from a place of acknowledging the primacy and power of the good. This very act of acknowledging the good is an assault on evil – a total rejection of it.

The Scriptures tell us that it takes the saving work of Christ to restore that which was lost as a consequence of the Fall. Gratitude was a part of that loss, so its complete restoration in our lives depends on the saving grace of God. However, as image-bearers of God, we have all been bestowed with the capacity to recognise and practise gratitude. That is why, in the biblical narrative, our posture of gratitude is not expected to disappear because of the Fall. Gratitude remains an essential part of being in God's image. The Fall did not destroy it. As created beings, we are still required to live our lives from a place of gratitude. When that isn't happening, it will be replaced with a self-absorbed and problem-oriented approach to life.

> 'The very act of acknowledging the good is an assault on evil.'

> 'As created beings, we are still required to live our lives from a place of gratitude. When that isn't happening, it will be replaced with a self-absorbed and problem-oriented approach to life.'

Paul articulates in his letter to the Christians in Rome how a refusal to acknowledge the glory of God (which is his power, goodness and beauty displayed in creation), to give him due thanksgiving, or to worship him, led humanity to be left to itself: 'For although they knew God, they neither glorified him as God nor gave thanks to him, but their thinking became futile and their foolish hearts were darkened' (Romans 1:21).

Human beings' refusal to acknowledge and give thanks to God and the resulting consequences of that refusal communicates two things. First, it demonstrates the fact that, despite the Fall, human beings have the capacity to give due recognition and gratitude to God and his goodness in creation. Second, the refusal to do so leads humanity to be preoccupied by that which is not good: they 'exchanged the glory of the immortal God for images made to look like a mortal human being' (Romans 1:23).

This indicates Paul's expectation that gratitude will continue to be the appropriate posture of humanity even after the Fall. This is not because the world is a perfect place – nor does it mean that maintaining a posture of gratitude will be free from challenges, of course. Rather, it is because gratitude, as the right posture, directs us to God and helps us respond and tackle evil from a place of freedom from its consequences.

In Romans 12:21, Paul tells the Romans, 'Do not be overcome by evil, but overcome evil with good.' The good has more power than evil. The tendency of fallen humanity is to engage evil with evil. Engaging evil with evil will put us under its spell. However, gratitude will empower us to face the negative – not from a position of defeat but with a constructive force which results in positive change, compelling people to see the good and calling the best out of them.

Being grateful gives depth to human life. It enables us to recognise the inherent value and significance of the world around us, acknowledging the truth and goodness in everything God has given us. There is harm in viewing the world with a utilitarian mindset, in terms of what it can do for us or give us. Once the good is acknowledged in creation, the question of God becomes unavoidable. The first reference point for people to know and think about God is creation. Therefore, when we encourage others to notice and acknowledge the good, we direct them to engage with that which communicates God's goodness.

Summarising our theological definition and its practical implications, we can say that gratitude is, first and foremost, an acknowledgement of the good.

- The good acknowledged is the good appreciated. We express our appreciation of the good when we acknowledge it.
- The good acknowledged is the good promoted. We promote the good when we are intentional in acknowledging it.
- The good acknowledged is the good internalised. We internalise the good, allowing it to inform and shape our thoughts, emotions and behaviours when we acknowledge it.

Acknowledging the good is informative and transformational.

Gratitude, according to this definition, has many implications, which we will examine later in the book. Once the good is acknowledged, it could be expressed in several ways:

- Verbal: 'Thank you' – expressing our appreciation.
- Attitudinal: We recognise and acknowledge the good in others, in our life and surroundings, and our attitude towards them changes, resulting in relational transformation at all levels.
- Altruistic: Initiating selfless actions to bring about good for others.

Defining gratitude as an acknowledgement of the good is not just saying that when and if you see the good, you acknowledge it. The rationale behind the definition is a conviction that the good, not evil, has primacy – the primary place – in the world. As such, the good has to be acknowledged first, not evil. The good has to inform our posture and relatedness in life, not evil. So, it is a call for a proactive engagement with life, recognising and acknowledging the good before we engage in tackling the bad. The good is our origin and our destination; so giving a prime place to good should be our posture in between the two.

Gratitude is not an occurrence, an event or a sporadic episode that happens when we are in a good mood. Nor is it merely our

Gratitude explored

> 'Gratitude is not an occurrence, an event or a sporadic episode that happens when we are in a good mood.'

response to the gifts we receive. It is our stance in life, the way we relate to God, humanity and the world. It is not saying thank you; it goes deeper than that. It is an outlook, a worldview or a perspective.

Consider the differences between saying thank you and a posture of gratitude:

Thank you	Gratefulness
A response (something done for us)	A posture (inner disposition, a mindset)
Instant (there and then, about something that happened)	A position (backed by theologically and socially informed decision)
Reactive (to what happened or was given or observed)	Proactive (intentional engagement)
Doesn't need much content (and doesn't go beyond what happened)	Continuously gathering and internalising content
Passive (it is not active engagement)	Pre-emptive
Conditional (when good things are happening)	Consistent (irrespective of what happens)
Expression (to what is felt inside)	Bedrock (the foundation from where expressions spring)
Respectful (culturally)	Transformative

The difference between 'thank you' and gratefulness

We have navigated the concept of gratitude through the varying lenses of psychology, sociology and theology to understand its origins, manifestations and implications within the human experience. We have explored gratitude's psychological and sociological dimensions, which consider gratitude from the perspective of its benefits, viewing it primarily as a behavioural phenomenon and a virtue that can be nurtured and developed over time. These disciplines situate gratitude within the realm of human behaviour and moral virtues, suggesting that it is a quality that individuals can actively cultivate and integrate into their lives through conscious effort and practice. Conversely, within the theological framework, gratitude is not conceptualised merely as a behaviour or virtue, but as an inherent aspect of human nature, albeit potentially dormant. The theological perspective positions gratitude as an integral element of humanity's essence, ingrained within the fabric of our existence as creatures.

We conclude this exploration of gratitude by listening in on a conversation with Miroslav Volf, Professor of Theology and Director of the Yale Center for Faith and Culture at Yale University, USA. In it, he reflects on the essence of gratitude, its effects on relationships, its role in transformation, its contribution to the common good and its connection to the primacy of goodness.[13]

In conversation with Professor Miroslav Volf

What does gratitude mean to you?
Personal gratitude seems to me to be a really important practice – and more than just a practice, it's a really important stance towards the world. As a Christian, I believe in what one might describe as the 'primordial goodness' of the world – in other words, that goodness is primary. If goodness is primary, and if it's goodness that comes from God, then

it is a gift from God. And, therefore, I think that my basic orientation in the world ought to be one of gratitude. It should be one of thanksgiving – almost in a way of receiving that very gift that is given to us with creation. To me, it's very important more generally as a stance in the world – but also individually, in terms of honouring gifts that one receives with gratitude.

How does gratitude change relational dynamics?
When one understands gratitude as a form of relationship that one has with another person or to a thing that another person has given, then this whole relationship between that person and the object transforms, and it changes. And I think we need to keep that in mind and also recognise that one purpose of giving gifts is not simply to enrich or benefit the person, but also to create a cycle of gift-giving. Then that person who receives the gift in turn becomes a giver. The places of gratitude and the gifts that they exchange start circulating. Many people have imagined God's Trinitarian life to be just such gift-giving exchanges, where we receive and where divine persons receive, and they give.

I always like to talk about how my father (who's now deceased) gave me a fountain pen. These are not appreciated these days so much because we don't write by hand, but it was a golden-nibbed fountain pen, a relatively simple one called a Pelican pen. I imagine that I could go somewhere, if I had money, and buy myself a much nicer fountain pen. And yet I would never prefer the nicer fountain pen to the one that my father gave me. Why is that? Because somehow my father is in that pen. When I have a relationship with that pen, I have a relationship with him. And if it's a gift from somebody who loves me or who I love I realise that this whole object becomes alive in a very different way. What was just an ordinary object becomes a sacrament in the presence of that other person.

Gratitude involves recognising the presence of God as the giver in both objects and people. This recognition transforms our perception, making these objects and people come alive to us in a unique and profound way. When we adopt an attitude of gratitude, we begin to see the world through a different lens, one that highlights the beauty and significance of everything around us. Thus, cultivating a stance of gratitude is fundamental to experiencing a truly flourishing life.

I would say we need two kinds of thing to flourish. We need to have material things. We are physical–biological beings and therefore we need to have things that will satisfy our basic needs. Maybe we need also a little bit more than that, because we are also cultural beings and not just physical beings. And the things that we need change, but we can identify the things we need.

But if we only have material things, they become almost dead to us. They become just 'things' to us. They have utility value, but we don't have affection for them. Whereas when we have something given as a gift (or when we relate to things in a certain way), we can come to feel almost at home with them – just like I feel at home with this fountain pen that my father gave me.

I believe that this relationship to the world is in fact what's significant for flourishing because it makes joy possible – and wonder and the beauty and kind of surprise in the world.

How does retrospective reflection help us embrace gratitude?
Sometimes we don't know what it is appropriate to be grateful for. Very often, if we are deeply introspective about our lives, the things we end up being grateful for are sometimes things which we didn't feel that we could be grateful for at the time they were happening. Retrospectively, we look back and we say: 'It's not the pain that I endured. It's not the suffering that I have undergone. It's not the persecution. It's not that these things are good in themselves. But, by the grace of God, they have been used to create something good. And I need to express that out of something that is not good, good has come. I am, in a sense, grateful that it happened. I am better off. The good has come to me. I'm better off for that having occurred.'

I know that this is not something a person can tell somebody else, right in the middle of the suffering. If we do that, it looks like, 'Oh, I'm this very smart, comfortable know-it-all who is telling the other person just be grateful for whatever it is.' That we cannot say, because we don't actually know how situations are. And we ought to honour and respect the pain and suffering people are undergoing.

But at the same time, we can be open to saying, retrospectively, 'Oh, I can be grateful for something that was very hard. Something arduous, something that demanded work of me and something that I unwillingly accepted. Something that I kicked and screamed against. But it became good, for which I'm grateful.'

How does gratitude facilitate the common good?
I think if we can identify the good, and if we can be grateful together, it means that we agree on some significant common

good. Common gratitude refers to things that we are grateful for and maybe the one we are grateful to. Maybe it is possible, even if we disagree as to whom we are grateful for, we can still be grateful for the same things. To the extent that we are in agreement of the 'goods' that we should celebrate and rejoice in, that already creates a bond, a communal bond. Out of the shared experience of goodness, it is possible to look for ways in which we might bridge gaps where gaps continue to exist.

I always thought that it was important – whether in interfaith relations or relations with people with whom we are strongly at odds – to identify what we share and the interests and goods that we have in common. Once we start from there, I think the conversation can then lead in the proper directions.

I recall a very simple saying that many people have used, but it's applicable here. The first time I heard it was from [Christian pastor and author] Rick Warren, I think, about the relationship among people of different faiths. He said that the building of relationships moves from hand to heart to head. Working together on something is like saying that we have something with which we are commonly concerned, something we both consider to be good. And gratitude can play that role in that initial process, as well as all along the entirety of that process.

How does gratitude help us create a space for transformation?
The Zacchaeus story is very, very fascinating and informing in this regard. And clearly, the accusation from the community didn't stop Zacchaeus from doing what he was doing. What strikes me in that story is, as in some other stories, that Jesus has eyes to see what other people do not see. In Luke's Gospel, chapter seven, the sinful woman comes and washes Jesus' feet.

And then Jesus is criticised by the host (who is scandalised) because a sinful woman has come into his house and Jesus is allowing her to wash his feet.

The question that Jesus asks Simon is, 'Do you see this woman?' And you can say, 'Well, of course he saw the woman because that's why he's complaining about it.' But then Jesus might repeat the question. 'Do you *really* see that woman, who she is?' And, in her case, this ability to *see* somebody, to recognise their humanity, recognise their goodness and their movement towards good, was picked up by Jesus. And she was freed.

I think something similar might be going on with Zacchaeus. There is a 'son of Abraham' and he is human. You can name various other things that might be there, that Jesus sees. Maybe Jesus also sees his discomfort with himself and with the chains that he has put upon himself. He can't tear them off and he needs some help – not accusatory help, but help to enhance his humanity so that he can be freed, the gift of grace so that he can be free.

And suddenly, by that very gift Jesus gives to him of *seeing* him, Zacchaeus is transformed. And he now wants to get rid of everything that he has wrongfully obtained and wants to give more to those he has harmed than what otherwise might be normal or equitable for him to do.

I see gift-giving and gratitude as key dynamics in this. As you suggested in your question, I think it can be also a dynamic in relationships as we engage with people who deeply disagree with us or with people who themselves seem to be captive to the powers of evil, out of which they cannot release themselves. But somewhere deep down, they long for that release.

How does the primacy of the good inform gratitude?
You can see in many ways that in Paul and in Jesus there's a primacy of the good. The good leads the way. And you can see that, especially in the ministry of Jesus, when the Gospel of Mark summarises the whole ministry of Jesus at the very beginning of the gospel: he came and he preached the *good* news. The good news was what the Christian faith was about – the good news of salvation that is coming and, therefore, something for which we are grateful as good news for us. It's not that there's no repentance there. It's not that there's no critique. It's there. But repentance is in the function of this good news because the good news is there. Therefore, I align my life from one direction towards the other direction, to that which is good.

I think we are motivated also by the good to transform our lives when we find ourselves in just ordinary situations. It's really important to me not to think that the first thing we need to do with the world is to critique it. The first thing that we need to do is to enhance the good in the world. Good is already there and needs to be enhanced, and more time and more effort should be spent on enhancing the good than on combating the bad.

That brings me to the role of gratitude. I feel that if you want to think about what priority gratitude or complaint should have, I would say that gratitude has priority. That's not to exclude the complaint.

Why does gratitude or the positive have primacy? I think it is probably best illustrated for me when I think about the famous speech that Martin Luther King made during the march to Washington. It was his 'I have a dream' speech. If he had given an 'I have a complaint' speech, I don't think too many would have followed him.

Now, he had a lot to complain about within that speech itself. It was a march for jobs. At stake was the ability of people to satisfy their basic needs to feed themselves and to feed their families. It was about jobs and freedom. At stake was the human dignity of these people. Nonetheless, he doesn't first lead with a complaint. Complaint is not fundamental to the speech. Fundamental is the dream that is there. Fundamental is the good that has to be created, that has to be enhanced.

That points in the direction that we need to go and the actions we need to take. We need the two elements, just like in Jesus' proclamation, good news and repentance. We also need gratitude and complaint – and the proper place of complaint (if it's properly executed) is essential. It's a critique. It's a way of turning from what isn't quite right. There's going to be a place for it as long as the Messiah does not come and the world doesn't become God's world, as it properly ought to be.

4

Gratitude misunderstood

We were surprised when Jacob stood up to challenge the decision of our CEO's announcement. What we'd heard had shocked us all, but none of the rest of us had been courageous enough to challenge the decision. Even Sarah, who was not afraid of confrontation and always had something to complain about, didn't say a word.

Jacob, known as 'Mr Positive' because of his tendency to talk about and highlight the positive even in a dire situation, never expected to speak. When he raised his hand to contribute, we all thought that he would endorse what the CEO had decided. As we expected, he started by talking about the strengths of the organisation, its contributions over the years and how progress had happened as a result of excellent leadership and a strong workforce.

As Jacob went on highlighting the strengths of the organisation, the rest of us were boiling with frustration and anger. At the far corner of the room, the two section managers whose jobs were directly affected by the decision were murmuring. It was easy to guess from their faces the content of the muttered conversations they were having while Jacob was talking. Their fury was clearly directed not only at the senior management, but also towards Jacob.

But once he'd finished narrating the company's strengths, with painstaking detail, Jacob changed tack. He started to present his argument as to why the decision of the senior management was untimely and unhelpful to the company's success. Observing how skilfully he articulated the argument and the number of points he raised to support it, we almost concluded that he must have had prior knowledge of the decision.

Gratitude misunderstood

Suddenly, the facial expressions of the management team started to show discomfort and apprehension. The rest of the room became glittered with smiles. The people who had wanted him to stop before certainly didn't want him to stop now – and vice versa.

When Jacob finished his argument, fully composed and with a smile, the management team didn't know how to respond. After a few minutes of deliberation, they reversed the decision and told us that they would find another way to tackle the problem.

We just couldn't believe what had happened. The dark cloud that had engulfed the room had now dispersed, and everybody was smiling, looking in Jacob's direction.

David, the loudest of all of us, said to Jacob, 'I thought when you started talking that you would drive the nail into the coffin. Where did this come from? I thought you were Mr Joyous, Mr Positive, prescribing gratitude for every situation. You became the opposite of that today.'

Jacob replied calmly, 'No, I didn't. I was acting in the same way I've always acted.'

Lola interrupted him and said, 'I must admit, I thought you talked about gratitude because you were weak and scared to face challenge or confrontation. Oh boy! How wrong was I!' We all laughed and admitted that we thought the same.

Not to lose the opportunity to push the benefits of gratitude one more time, Jacob started by agreeing with us. He said, 'I don't blame you. We were taught to think that gratitude is a weak posture which naively endorses bad situations and doesn't have the backbone to speak truth to power. But that is a big misconception. Being grateful and telling the truth to power are compatible. We consider reacting, focusing on the problem and starting our conversation with highlighting wrongs as a strength, but it is not. What happened today was a good example.

'We all were upset with the decision. We knew the management team hadn't bothered to consider other ways to fix the problem. But we were not able to speak, in my opinion, for two reasons. First, we knew that if we spoke, our emotions would get the better of us and we would say something we might later regret. Second, we were so angry that we were not able to think clearly enough to articulate our arguments. I was in the same position but decided not to let one wrong decision overshadow the many good things we had in the company. In the process, I started to feel calmer and composed and was able to think clearly.

'Starting my argument by acknowledging the good had the same effect in the minds of the management team. They were happy and felt proud as I listed the successes of the organisation. When I started to present my reasons why their decision should be reversed, they didn't feel disrespected or consider my argument as an attack directed at them. So, it was easy for them to see the strength of my argument.'

Looking around at the faces of his friends as he was finishing his last sentence, Jacob thought to himself that he'd never had their attention in the way he did that day.

Dispelling misconceptions

Jacob's story is a relatable experience for many who have embraced gratitude as a guiding principle. And his journey also reflects the societal perception of gratitude as a sign of weakness, a coping mechanism to evade reality's harsh truths. It is a poignant illustration of the misunderstandings surrounding gratitude.

When I share gratitude as a framework, the initial responses I receive are often negative. The arguments tend to go like this: 'Why grateful? There are lots of wrongs, injustices and inequalities happening around us. What we need is justice, equality and a change of mindset – not gratitude. What is there to be grateful about? Grateful for what? Gratitude is a soft approach which refuses to see the wrongs. It will give people the wrong idea and let them feel that they've been right all along. It goes against our struggle.'

I acknowledge that gratitude will not always result in our preferred outcomes. However, when people first said things like that to me, I didn't appreciate where the problem lay. I was trying to respond to questions, but I wasn't able to convince people until I realised where the misunderstanding was coming from. The problem is how we understand gratitude. If our basic understanding of gratitude is different, then it isn't surprising if we differ in our understanding of the potential outcomes.

Contrary to common assumptions, gratitude builds bridges, overcomes barriers and transforms relationships. It emboldens us to speak the truth and correct the wrongs. Primarily, it helps us see in others their worthiness in the eyes of a loving God, despite their weaknesses.

> 'Gratitude builds bridges, overcomes barriers and transforms relationships.'

Gratitude is often misunderstood, commonly viewed to be a sign of weakness, inferiority and ingratiation. It is seen as transactional, hierarchical, and is sometimes perceived as a killer of ambition and a resigned acceptance of circumstances. Some regard it as naive or soft, potentially overlooking injustice and being hesitant to speak truthfully.

Gratitude as weakness

The misconception that gratitude is a weakness is prevalent in today's competitive and individualistic Western society. In a culture that prioritises self-promotion and personal gain, the act of acknowledging and celebrating the strengths of others can be seen as a weakness or an obstacle to personal advancement. Overlooking the profound impact of gratitude on mental, emotional and relational well-being, this type of climate encourages individuals to promote themselves and, where necessary, exploit the weaknesses of others.

Moreover, viewing gratitude as a weakness contradicts our admiration for individuals who, despite facing significant obstacles, have become forces for good by choosing not to respond negatively to their challenges. These individuals focus on the small positives, even when it would be natural to dwell on the negatives. The alternative – focusing on wrongs, being dominated by negative feelings and acting out accordingly – would not have led to the impactful outcomes that make us remember them. We respect their ability to control their natural reactions and guide themselves towards their preferred outcomes and lasting solutions. We regard them as strong, not weak, because they overcome the temptation to respond negatively and instead act with love or forgiveness, recognising and prioritising the good. Their ability to see the good amid the bad is a sign of courage, a form of defiance that exposes the flaws in negative responses. Therefore, gratitude, as an acknowledgement of the good and a conviction in the power of the good, is far from a weakness.

Considering gratitude as a weakness arises from a perception that it would not be an effective posture to have in the current competitive and individualistic society. However, this conclusion fails to appreciate how gratitude actually serves our personal interests, while also serving the interests of others. If we are solely concerned with our own personal interests, that not only leads to unhappiness but also to difficulties in our relationships. Self-absorption is the root cause of sin and is always counterproductive.

Gratitude as transactional

We are living in a time when everything is measured by its transactional value: 'What will I get from this?' We do things as

Gratitude misunderstood

a response to the good we receive or because of the transactional value that it will have for us in the long run.

There is nothing wrong in responding with gratitude to the benefits we receive or acting in a way that will add value for us. The problem is when we measure or base our relationships and interactions with the world *only* in transactional terms.

When we understand gratitude in transactional terms – 'I'll be grateful because of what I'll get out of the process' – we underplay its wider implications. Yes, it is appropriate to be grateful and express our gratitude when good is done to us or when we witness good being done to others. However, when we understand and practise gratitude as a transaction, we wait for the good to happen to us first. This quickly becomes a passive engagement with gratitude, and in the absence of good done to us, we cease to practise it. In this mode, gratitude loses its ability to help us overcome negative emotions and elevate us above our problems. We also miss out on the challenge it gives us to find a fresh perspective on our situation.

Gratitude clears our vision as we go through the storms of life. It is not a passive trait where we wait for something good to happen before we express it. It is an active engagement in recognising the good, with the conviction that the good has primacy in the world.

> 'Gratitude clears our vision as we go through the storms of life.'

When we economise gratitude and see it as a transactional currency, we put the burden of being good onto other people, awaiting their action before taking any of our own. If we constantly position ourselves as recipients rather than givers, we will end up with unfulfilled (and unreasonable) expectations that, in time, will permanently affect our view of others. Limiting gratitude to a mere acknowledgement of the good that has been received drastically restricts the profound impact it can have on our lives and the lives of others.

A grateful response to the good we receive is, of course, appropriate. But true gratitude doesn't wait for the good to come. It seeks it out.

> 'True gratitude doesn't wait for the good to come. It seeks it out.'

Gratitude as hierarchical

Another misunderstanding about the nature of gratitude lies in the notion that it is inherently hierarchical, putting the one who expresses gratitude in a lower position than the one who receives it. The weak says thank you to the strong, or the poor thanks the rich – as if being grateful is an instrument used by the strong and the rich to keep the weak and the poor in their place. Gratitude in this context is seen as an act of embracing an inferior position in society.

Any truth, concept or principle can of course be abused and misused – and gratitude is no different. When gratitude is demanded or the result of coercion, it is no longer true gratitude. However, gratitude willingly expressed and practised out of a recognition of the good, out of an individual's freedom and personal conviction, shouldn't be labelled as hierarchical. The grateful person acting in this way is not functioning under the influence of others but from their own belief of what is good. Therefore, they are operating outside of the hierarchy that others would impose on them.

Gratitude as toxic positivity

Sometimes gratitude is labelled as 'toxic positivity'.[1] The suggestion is that an overly optimistic attitude can blind individuals to life's harsh realities. However, true gratitude does not shy away from looking adversity full in the face. In fact, it empowers us to confront challenges with resilience and hope. By fostering a mindset focused on abundance rather than scarcity, gratitude enables individuals to navigate life's complexities with courage and creativity.

Gratitude misunderstood

Gratitude is not 'toxic positivity' that naively expects the negative to disappear if I continue to be positive. Shying away from the negative, being foolishly optimistic, responding with false assurances rather than being realistic – all this comes from feeling uncomfortable about negative emotions. Gratitude is far from those kinds of worldviews or behaviours. Gratitude embraces negative emotions but doesn't allow them to determine the outcome of or the approach to a situation. Gratitude is a force that empowers us to engage with life's difficulties from a place of freedom and strength. It doesn't encourage us to shy away from challenges – it empowers us to face them.

Having examined the multifaceted misconceptions surrounding gratitude that characterise it as weak, transactional, hierarchical or even toxic, we now turn to Dr Harvey Kwiyani's perspective on the true essence of gratitude.[2] He explains the place of gratitude in Ubuntu life philosophy as a catalyst for human connection and revitalisation within diverse communities. In particular, he highlights how the reciprocal exchange of gifts is essential for the growth and vitality of the collective body.

In conversation with Dr Harvey Kwiyani

I'm an African, from Malawi. And I am of Bantu heritage. There are probably half a billion of us Bantus scattered across sub-Saharan Africa, especially from Cameroon to Kenya, Uganda and then down to South Africa. Quite a few hundred tribal communities with very many shared cultural heritages. So, our languages are somewhat related. When I'm in Kenya, for example, sometimes I find myself in a place where I don't need a translator. I will understand 20, 30 or 40% of what's being said, because the words are similar. So, there are quite a lot of things that we share as Bantu peoples.

Gratitude misunderstood

We, as Bantus, are home to a life philosophy that's called Ubuntu – the word Bantu is the root for what is known as Ubuntu. Ubuntu became popular in the nineties after the fall of apartheid in South Africa. It was a time when South African political leaders and theologians began to articulate a new way of living for the South African community that, in the words of Desmond Tutu, required that people forgive one another. But that forgiveness would not happen if people did not realise that they were all human. And, of course, as Desmond Tutu would say, there's no future without forgiveness.

But to get to a place where we can forgive one another, we need to understand that we are all human. And to be human means you belong to the human community. As a resource for that conversation in South Africa, they had to go to Ubuntu because Ubuntu says: 'I am because we are. I cannot exist in isolation. Because I belong, therefore I am.' The community is made up of each individual. Individuals make the community. But in reverse, the community turns around and makes the individuals.

> 'I am because we are. I cannot exist in isolation. Because I belong, therefore I am.'

Without this dynamic between the individual and the community, there is no community. And because there's no community, there is also no individual. Because I am, because I belong and because I need my community to shape me, it means that for this to work, we need to have human relations that will keep both the community and the individual functions.

The bottom line for us as Bantu peoples then is to say that gratitude is the thing that makes this interrelation dynamic happen. That makes the individual the individual, but also makes the individual somebody who contributes to the community, and then makes the community something that shapes the individual. It happens because of gratitude. So, my argument here is that it's gratitude that makes humanity possible. Without gratitude, we run the risk of being isolationists and enemies forever.

Gratitude allows us to be able to see one another – and see one another not just because I can see you (you are standing right in front of me), but seeing in the sense that I recognise that you're here and I recognise you. South Africans, again, will say for greeting, '*Sawubona*', which simply means, 'We see you.' It means, 'I recognise that you're here. I recognise that you're human. You're human enough to have my attention. You're human enough to make me stop what I'm doing to pay attention to the fact that you are here. I see you.' And that requires gratitude.

In this twenty-first century, we know for sure that God has Christians in every part of the world. Every country has a Christian presence. All those Christian communities have something unique that only those communities can bring to the body of Christ. And they need to have something unique; otherwise, they're just repeating something that's being said somewhere else. They need to have something authentic that God has given to them and only to them to bring to the table.

Ephesians 4:16 says that the church body is glued together by that which every joint supplies. *Every joint* has something to supply. It's the mutual exchange between the members that makes the body. Without the mutual exchange between the members, the body is weak, the body is not functional. There has to be a mutual exchange – a giving and receiving. Each one of us – it doesn't matter what your financial status is, it doesn't matter where you come from – but each one of us has something to give and something to receive.

I do know that some cultures are good at giving but not receiving. And I know that some cultures are good at receiving but not giving. But within the body, we give and we receive. This is where Ubuntu becomes helpful, because Ubuntu says that what makes me is both what God has given me and what God has given me through the people that I am with. It says that I don't have everything I need – and that's by design. God made it that way. At the end of the day, I have to need my community. I have to need somebody. And, in reverse, that which God has given me will help shape the body. It will help make this thing that God wants to do in the world happen.

I have a duty to receive. I don't have everything I need. I'm not self-sufficient, I'm not self-contained; there's only one self-sufficient being in this world and it's God. I don't have everything I need. And it's OK. It's because God has shaped me to be in a community with others. What I need, a part of it has been given to the people around me to make me what God wants me to be. And my friends, my neighbours – in the same way, I have something that God has given me that is not for me; it's for them. Therefore, it's the exchange between what God has given me for my neighbours and what God has given my neighbours for me that makes this community happen.

That's what Ubuntu says. Nelson Mandela talked about how strangers are treated when they come into a community in a typical Ubuntu setting (and that's not even a Christian setting), and he gave an example of a stranger who walks into a village at sunset. The village knows that if this stranger is allowed to proceed on his journey, five miles down the road he will meet lions and they will kill him. And so, the village has to persuade this stranger for their humanity to spend the night, because if he is killed five miles down the road, it reflects on their personhood, on their Ubuntu.

And this is all happening because, in a typical Ubuntu understanding, you believe that there is a spirit world, probably of God, that is orchestrating all these meetings. This stranger who comes here doesn't just come by accident. There is the hand of God somewhere in this. And maybe this stranger brings the very thing that we need to resolve some of our issues here because he's coming into this community with a fresh set of eyes. He will see our problems in a different light and things will begin to change. You have to be hospitable.

In this context, then, when the stranger walks into this village, the village has no other choice but to be grateful that this stranger is here. He could have gone anywhere else, but God, the spirit and the ancestors have brought him into this village. There must be something. They may celebrate the fact that this stranger is an engineer – he's going to help them figure out the water situation in the village. But they have to be grateful for the person themselves, not just the gift that they bring. It's not the knowledge, it's not the giftings. It's the person – the coming of this person here among us is something that we have to be grateful for.

And why is that important? It's important because God has designed the body to function through the exchange. We know from the sciences that homogeneity is a slow death. That's why the gene pools have to keep mixing. You don't marry your sister. You have to be married to somebody else and keep the gene pool mixing to avoid this slow death.

God uses diversity to revitalise God's work in the world. We cannot talk about Christianity in Europe today without appreciating the presence of many Christians who have come from around the world and are doing their faith here, living among us. And it is through this diversity that God begins to revitalise British Christianity.

Back in the 1800s, British missionaries were going to Africa. I'm a direct descendant of people who were converted by the very first missionaries in Malawi in the 1860s. It is important for us as British Christians to grasp this history, to hear and understand, because we cannot talk about mission history without recognising the work that Britain did – whether it's David Livingstone or Hudson Taylor or William Carey or Robert Moffat or Mary Slessor. British work in world mission cannot be overestimated. It is because of their foundations that we have world Christianity today, that we celebrate the fact that there are Christians in every country in the world. Britain has played a huge part in that story.

Now, of course we can celebrate that. Yes, there are many Presbyterians in Malawi – more than in the Church of Scotland itself. We can be happy about that. We can talk about how the Nigerian Anglican community, the Church of Nigeria, is larger than the Anglican communion in Europe and North America put together. We can celebrate that.

But we need to move beyond that. We need to begin to see that what happened there in those other parts of the world has found its way back here to the West. We can't just celebrate and recognise British missionary work in Africa without recognising the fruit of that work that has come back to be with us here. That's important.

Back then, the missionaries used to say, 'There is going to come a day when people from Africa, Asia and Latin America are going to come to Britain to reinvigorate British Christianity.' That 'day' is now!

The challenge for us is that we find it difficult to receive the very gifts those people bring. We have a problem processing them and accepting how they would work in a British context. But beyond that, we have problems receiving those Christians as a gift to us.

I am a gift to this place. The way I would explain Ubuntu theology as a basis for gratitude could only come from somebody from my part of Africa. That's a gift that I bring. And it's the receiving of the gifts that are brought to us and the receiving of the people whom God has brought as gifts to us that will make a difference. Ephesians 4:8 says that when Jesus went up to heaven, he 'gave gifts to his people'. And of course, the gifts are the people, the apostles, the evangelists. He gave them as gifts to men and women.

Today, God has given the British church gifts of Nigerians, Jamaicans, Ghanaians, South Africans and so on. And that is something to be grateful for. Walter Hollenweger, a Swiss-German theologian at Birmingham University, once said that British Christians prayed for revival. When it came, they did not recognise it because it was black. And I add that it was black and Pentecostal. God has brought us gifts. Let's be grateful for them. It's gratefulness, it's gratitude, that will unlock those gifts that will then strengthen this body that God is building in Britain.

5

The biblical and theological foundation of the gratitude way

Give thanks in all circumstances; for this is God's will for you in Christ Jesus.
(1 Thessalonians 5:18)

This verse is a tough one to digest while going through a difficult time. However, in every facet of our lives, regardless of the circumstances we encounter, it is paramount to cultivate a spirit of thankfulness. This practice not only resonates with God's will, as outlined in the verse above, but it also fosters a deeper connection with our faith and spirituality. Even in the midst of adversity, when the weight of trials and tribulations threatens to overwhelm us, adhering to this principle can be profoundly transformative.

We can all learn from the poignant example of Son Yang-Won, a venerable Korean pastor whose life epitomises the remarkable influence of gratitude in the face of insurmountable challenges. From 1938 to 1941, he served as pastor at Ae-yan-won leper colony in South Korea, resuming ministry after four years in prison.

Despite enduring the hardships of colonial oppression and grappling with personal tragedies, Son Yang-Won remained steadfast in his commitment to spreading love and ministering to his community. His unwavering dedication and selflessness serve as a testament to the enduring power of faith amid adversity. One particularly heart-breaking moment in Son Yang-Won's narrative is his response to the tragic loss of two of his sons, who were martyred for their beliefs. Rather than yielding to despair or bitterness, Son

The biblical and theological foundation

Yang-Won chose to offer a prayer of gratitude at their funeral, a gesture that speaks volumes about his unwavering faith and trust in a higher purpose.

In this act of profound spiritual fortitude, Son Yang-Won demonstrated his conviction that even in the face of unimaginable loss, there exists a divine plan that transcends human understanding. By imitating the example set forth by Son Yang-Won, we are reminded of the transformative potential inherent in the practice of gratitude. It is through appropriately expressing thanks, even in the midst of life's greatest trials, that we not only acknowledge God's sovereignty but also elevate ourselves above the challenges that threaten to engulf us. In doing so, we bring glory to God and inspire others to embrace a similar ethos of resilience and faith.

Here is the prayer of Nine Thanks offered by Revd Son Yang-Won at the funeral service of his two sons who were martyred by a mob of rebels.[1]

1. I thank the Lord for producing sons of martyrdom from the blood for a sinner like me.
2. I thank the Lord for choosing me, among so many believers, to have the privilege of caring for these beautiful treasures.
3. I thank the Lord for letting me offer up my eldest and my second eldest sons, the most beloved of three boys and three girls.
4. They say it is precious to have a son who is martyred. Still more, I thank the Lord that my two sons were martyred together.
5. They say it is blessing [enough] to believe in Jesus and die a peaceful death, but I thank the Lord for letting my sons be shot to death while carrying out the work of evangelism.

6 My sons were preparing to study abroad in the U.S., but I thank the Lord, because my heart is relieved to know that they went to heaven, a better place than America.
7 I thank the Lord for giving me a loving heart with which to lead my enemy to repentance and embrace him as my son.
8 I am thankful because I believe that the martyrdom of my two sons will bear countless fruits of heaven.
9 I thank the Lord for allowing me to recognize God's love even in adversity and for granting me faith to overcome.

Anchoring gratitude in biblical and theological accounts

Gratitude is a posture that helps us transcend the challenging circumstances that might discourage us. It also keeps us grounded during the good times that could make us forget the true source of our blessings. As we continue our exploration of gratitude, we now delve deeper into the foundational biblical narratives. The inherent goodness prevalent since the genesis of creation highlights the fundamental importance of acknowledging and embracing gratitude as an integral aspect of existence. Our journey begins in the creation narrative and in the gospel, which reveals the precedence of both goodness and gratitude. We then navigate the pathways of gratitude as explained in Paul's letters, in the book of Revelation, in the transformative power of *shalom* in Jeremiah 29, and in the theological concepts of the Trinity, ecclesiology and eschatology – as well as considering the catastrophic effects of ingratitude. As we do so, we see how goodness and gratitude are the golden threads woven through the entirety of the biblical narrative. The key points are summarised at the start of each section.

Goodness in creation

- In Genesis, goodness exists before evil. It plays a key role in how we understand and interact with God, other people and the world.
- Even after humanity's fall into sin, the world still reflects God's goodness and glory, showing that goodness endures.
- If we overlook the importance of goodness, we allow evil to affect our thoughts and shape how we view life.

Creation comes from our good God, out of his loving kindness. God himself approved the goodness of creation: 'And God saw that it was good'.[2] He also communicated his goodness to all creation in the act and process of creation. Therefore, we can say that the goodness of God is intrinsic to creation and constitutes its basic identity. The root of that goodness doesn't originate from anywhere else but the goodness of the Creator. The life of human beings on earth started on the sixth day as God created Adam, then Eve. The very next day, on the Sabbath, they rested with God, admiring, celebrating, enjoying and acknowledging his goodness to them in creation.

We understand from the Scriptures that the good came first and, as such, it has a primal place in the world. As well as that, despite the Fall, nature retains its transcendental truth, goodness and beauty. In chapter 5 of his epistle to the Romans, Paul explains how evil entered the good world that God originally created. He refers to the Genesis narrative, highlighting the pivotal moment when sin, synonymous with evil, entered the human experience through the actions of one man, Adam. This act of disobedience against God's command marked the beginning of sin in the world. Consequently, sin brought death, resulting in not just physical demise but also a broader spectrum of destruction and decay. Through this theological reflection, Paul emphasises sin's role as a

The biblical and theological foundation

destructive force that seeks to dismantle the goodness embedded in the world by God. However, the intrusion of evil did not eradicate the presence of good. The beauty and intricate design of nature, as well as the love, compassion and kindness found in humanity and the animal kingdom, demonstrates the enduring presence of good in the world.

And the goodness of God still shines through creation. In Isaiah 6, we witness this truth in the declaration of the angels – the truth that the earth is full of the glory of God. They declare, 'Holy, holy, holy is the Lord Almighty; the whole earth is full of his glory' (Isaiah 6:3). God's glory is his presence, power, beauty and goodness. One expects God's glory to encompass a multitude of divine attributes that reflect his essence. For our discussion, his glory is evident in the magnificence of the natural world and the depth of his love that permeates his interactions with humanity and his creation.

Psalm 8 also communicates the glory, power, wisdom and goodness of God throughout creation and humanity:

> Lord, our Lord,
>   how majestic is your name in all the earth!
> You have set your glory
>   in the heavens...
> When I consider your heavens,
>   the work of your fingers,
> the moon and the stars,
>   which you have set in place,
> what is mankind that you are mindful of them,
>   human beings that you care for them?
> (Psalm 8:1, 3–4)

Therefore, despite the persistent presence of evil, and its insistence that it should attain a primal place in our worldview, the Scriptures

The biblical and theological foundation

invite us to acknowledge first the goodness of God in the world. When we decide to do this, we overcome the occupying insistence of evil, its dominance over our soul and perspective. We can engage with evil from a place of freedom, rather than from its prison cell. The primal acknowledgement of the good is free to dictate our relatedness, our behaviour and interactions in the world – not evil.

After the Fall, the disastrous change that took place lay in the fact that the knowledge of evil, or wrong, took primary position in the mind of humanity and creation. This affected the way humans see and relate to creation as well as to their Creator. Human relations, starting from the first family in the biblical story, inform us that the outworking of sin is to make human beings gravitate to evil, rather than to the good.

As a product of human behaviour and tendency, our Western culture doesn't encourage us to focus and talk about the good around us, in our lives and in others. Instead, the news in many media outlets focuses on the negative things happening in our world, on our weaknesses and the faults of others. Few people are interested in communicating the numerous good things happening in our communities. As a result, thinking and giving the good a primary place becomes hard work and, at times, is seen as foolishness or being indifferent to the evil around us.

> 'The news in many media outlets focuses on the negative things happening in our world.'

However, failure to acknowledge the primary place of the goodness and glory of God in creation has led humanity to focus on evil, facilitating its occupation of our mind. That is what we see in Romans 1. The refusal to acknowledge God's attributes and power in creation and a failure to give due honour to God resulted from a preoccupation with worthless thinking, leading humanity to deeper wickedness. In the process, what was destroyed was humanity's relationship with God, itself, others and creation as a whole.

The biblical and theological foundation

...because that which is known about God is evident within them [in their inner consciousness], for God made it evident to them. For ever since the creation of the world His invisible attributes, His eternal power and divine nature, have been clearly seen, being understood through His workmanship [all His creation, the wonderful things that He has made], so that they [who fail to believe and trust in Him] are without excuse and without defense. For even though they knew God [as the Creator], they did not honor Him as God or give thanks [for His wondrous creation]. On the contrary, they became worthless in their thinking [godless, with pointless reasonings, and silly speculations], and their foolish heart was darkened.
(Romans 1:19–21 AMP)

Goodness preceded evil and asserted its central position in shaping our perceptions and interactions with humanity and the world. And, despite the Fall, the earth continues to reflect the goodness and glory of God, and the enduring nature of goodness, informing us of the primacy of the good.

The primacy of good in the gospel

- The gospel is good news, highlighting the inherent worth of humanity.
- Humans are created in God's image, making us so valuable that Christ sacrificed himself for our sins – an indication of God's great love for us.
- Therefore, the gospel promotes the way of gratitude, shaping our attitude to mission.

The gospel informs us of the primacy of the good by highlighting the worthiness of those who need saving: 'For God so loved the world that he gave his one and only Son, that whoever believes in him shall not perish but have eternal life. For God did not send his Son into the world to condemn the world, but to save the world through him' (John 3:16–17).

From God's perspective, there is good in the world that is worth dying for. The gospel is, first, good news, and it is due to the coming or the announcement of this good news that repentance is called for – not the other way around. The primary place of announcing the coming of the good doesn't prevent the call for repentance. It doesn't turn a blind eye to the wrong. In the presence of the good, the bad stands truly naked. Therefore, the gospel informs us that we should approach humanity not from a place of disgust at its sinfulness, but by recognising its worthiness to be saved as a divine image-bearer.

The gospel not only highlights the primacy of the good but also informs our missional approach. It affirms and recognises the worthiness of a human being, helping us to be reverent in its presence and operate from a place of divine love. Often our evangelism strategy tends to make what is missing, wrong or sinful in the life of individuals and communities the starting point or point of entry to our gospel conversations. As society gets answers for some of its struggles and challenges, we are pushed to the fringes, trying to find what is left unanswered, as if the gospel has no voice to speak through and to the strength of our community.

Gratitude in line with the gospel calls us to start by affirming the worth of humanity, by being an act and a posture of generosity to our neighbours and community, and living in the reality of the resurrection of Jesus Christ and creativity of the Spirit of God. It starts by restoring our creatureliness and highlighting the power, goodness and beauty of God in creation. Then, from God's beauty in creation, the gospel transits to the beauty of God himself revealed through the person of Jesus Christ.

The giftedness of life in Paul's letters

- In his letters, Paul teaches us that life is a gift.
- This perspective changes our outlook and improves our attitude to life.

The Corinthian church was a diverse congregation, comprising Jews and Gentiles, rich and poor, and both educated and uneducated individuals, mirroring the city's diversity. Despite their shared faith in Christ, the issues of division, segregation and class present in Corinth persisted within the church. Paul wrote his first letter to address these challenges and others. He warns them not to be 'inflated with pride in favor of one person over against another' (1 Corinthians 4:6, NABRE), comparing two specific people. Their pride reflects a lack of proper perspective – a lack of gratitude.[3] Paul proposes an attitude of gratitude as a solution. He starts by asking three rhetorical questions that have a theological reach far beyond the Corinthians.

- Who makes you different from anyone else?
- What do you have that you didn't receive?
- So, if you received it, why do you boast as though you didn't?

By these rhetorical questions, Paul is trying to help them regain the right perspective, which then leads them to humble thanksgiving.

In his immediate view, Paul is thinking of the gifts with which the Corinthians have been endowed, the gift of faith first of all, but then the charismatic gifts he introduced in the first chapter (1 Corinthians 1:4–7), and finally the gift of the series of preachers and teachers they have received. The teachers the Corinthians were boasting about were really just people whose job was passing on the gift God had given them. The boasting temper implied forgetfulness of this fact. Paul is not trying to prevent them from

The biblical and theological foundation

admiring or appreciating their spiritual leaders. Rather, he wants them to do it within the boundaries allowed by the Scriptures.[4] However, the Corinthians went beyond that boundary and boasted as if they had not received them from God. In this scenario, as theologian Gordon Fee points out, Paul argues that 'there are no grounds for anyone exulting oneself over another since any differences are ultimately attributed to God'.[5] Rather, they should remember that everything is a gift and that nothing is earned or deserved. Therefore, those who experience grace should live from an attitude of infinite gratitude.[6]

In a broader sense, according to Paul, the right view of life recognises that life and all within it is a gift. If we recognise life as a gift, then our stance in the world becomes that of gratitude.

> 'If we recognise life as a gift, then our stance in the world becomes that of gratitude.'

Paul's first question to the Corinthians is this: 'For who makes you different from anyone else?' (4:7). In other words, the origin of your difference does not come from you – it is not what you are or what you have. It is God who has made you different – just as he made others different. If you recognise your difference as a gift, you will be quick to recognise the difference of the other as a gift. Then, difference becomes a cause for grateful celebration, rather than a cause for contention.

> 'If you recognise your difference as a gift ... [it] becomes a cause for grateful celebration, rather than a cause for contention.'

His second question is this: 'What do you have that you did not receive?' (4:7). We need to take a long pause before we answer this question. In the process, we will discover the giftedness of life. The answer is simple: nothing! All is a gift! If all is a gift, the natural response should be a posture of gratitude.

Paul wants us to understand the giftedness of life, to acknowledge the interdependence of human life (to appreciate the contribution of others to where we are today) and our creatureliness (our limitations). This is a path to humility – and in the process of answering this question, all our pride will be deconstructed. This is a bridge between the natural and the spiritual, because if we start to acknowledge the giftedness of life and develop an attitude of gratitude, the question of God becomes inevitable.

Paul's third question is, 'If you did receive it, why do you boast as though you did not?' (4:7). Paul is saying to the Corinthians: if you had truly understood the giftedness of life and embraced a posture of gratitude, there wouldn't have been room for division, superiority or pride among you. The recognition of the giftedness of life will lead us to gratitude, not boasting.

The practice of gratitude in Paul's writing

- As Paul teaches and encourages Christian communities, he encourages the practice of gratitude.
- There were plenty of issues and difficulties he could have raised straightaway, but he chose to start with gratitude, appreciation and thanks.
- Focusing on their strengths enables these believers to have hope and courage to get things right in the future.

Gratitude is also used as a constructive approach in the New Testament to admonish, correct or handle difficulties in a relationship. It was a common approach for Paul, when he wrote to individuals or churches, to start by appreciating and acknowledging their strengths or the good among them and in them, before he tackled or rebuked them about the wrongs done. 'I thank God for you' is a typical opening sentence in Paul's letters.[7] Although God is praised as the ultimate source of the good among the congregation, their contribution as a church is implicit in Paul's letters. In other words, Paul expresses his gratitude to God about them so that they 'overhear' his gratitude. His first letter to the Corinthian church is a good example of this.

The church in Corinth was in a difficult situation. His information about their difficulties came partly from the household of Chloe. This family had told Paul that there were divisions and cliques in the church (1 Corinthians 1:11). He also had a letter from the church with questions on marriage and celibacy (1 Corinthians 7:1). The division, the case of incest, sexual impurity and quarrelsome spirits that led some to take their brothers and sisters to court were also among the issues he tackled in his letter.[8] In response to the questions raised by the church, he clarified their confusions about marriage and celibacy, about food offered to idols, order in conducting public worship and exercising spiritual gifts. Finally, he challenged those believers in the church who denied that the dead would rise.[9]

Having in mind all these tendencies, practices and beliefs in the church of Corinth, Paul would have been justified in engaging straightaway with the issues, rebuking and exposing the wrong practices in the church listed above.[10] However, he deliberately started by drawing a positive picture and highlighting the good among them due to the grace of God and the possibilities this grace had created for them. He always thanked God for them, for the grace given to them in Christ. Because of this grace, they were enriched in everything, 'with all kinds of speech and with all knowledge' (1:5).[11] The outworking of this grace resulted in the confirmation of the authenticity of the testimony of Christ among them. They would not lack any spiritual gift as they eagerly waited for the second coming of Christ. God would strengthen them to the end and make them stand before him blameless. In New Testament scholar Richard Hays' words, 'Paul portrays the Corinthians as important players in a grand story scripted by God'.[12]

The biblical and theological foundation

In the light of what is to come in the rest of the letter, it seems as though he is writing to a church that is thriving and faithful, helped by the grace received. Indeed, the first readers of the letter could easily assume as much.[13] It is clear that Paul is not interested just in exposing the violations of God's law, without any hope for a comeback. Instead, he sets a direction and articulates why redemption is a possibility before he exposes and discusses the wrongs committed. Besides, Paul's theology is clear that, as Gordon Fee puts it, 'in every redeemed person there is evidence of the grace of God, and that brings forth Paul's gratitude, both to God and for them'.[14]

Despite the wrongs done and the mistakes made, there is a strength in these new believers which they need to recognise in order to have hope and courage for correction. Paul presented that strength in the bundle of gratitude.

This trend of Paul is reflected in his letters to other churches and individuals:[15]

- To the church of Rome, 'First, I thank my God through Jesus Christ for all of you, because the news of your faith is being reported in all the world' (Romans 1:8).
- To the churches in Ephesus, 'I have not stopped giving thanks for you, remembering you in my prayers' (Ephesians 1:16).
- To the church in Philippi, 'I thank my God every time I remember you. In all my prayers for all of you, I always pray with joy, because of your partnership in the gospel from the first day until now' (Philippians 1:3–5).
- To the churches in Colossae, 'We always thank God, the Father of our Lord Jesus Christ, when we pray for you, because we have heard of your faith in Christ Jesus and of the love you have for all God's people – the faith and love that spring from the hope stored up for you in heaven' (Colossians 1:3–5).
- To the churches in Thessalonica, 'We ought always to thank

God for you, brothers and sisters, and rightly so, because your faith is growing more and more, and the love all of you have for one another is increasing' (2 Thessalonians 1:3).

In his letters to those churches, Paul had false teachings to correct, wrong behaviours to challenge and new commands to give, but he always led with the good that God had brought about in their communities.

Gratitude in Jesus' messages to the seven churches of Revelation

- In his message to the churches, Jesus starts by recognising and commending the positive aspects of their faith and life.
- The deliberate choice to recognise and affirm the good first shows a profound understanding of the transformative power of gratitude.

Jesus' messages to the seven churches of Revelation also reflect the gratitude approach. While on the island of Patmos, John receives revelations that include Jesus' messages to the seven churches in Asia. Among those churches, some had adopted beliefs and behaviours that were not in line with God's kingdom. Even though some of these churches warranted severe admonitions, Jesus still began with where God was at work through people's faithfulness.

In the case of the church in Ephesus, it was 'your deeds, your hard work and your perseverance'; he acknowledges and praises their intolerance of 'wicked people' and the fact that they 'hate the practices of Nicolaitans, which I also hate' (Revelation 2:1–3, 6). Nevertheless, the warning given to the church in Ephesus indicates the seriousness of their error. If the church did not repent and return to its first love, Christ would remove its lampstand, which signified the destruction of the church.

The biblical and theological foundation

In favour of the wisdom of the gratitude approach for correction, there seems to be more praise for Ephesus and Thyatira, which are rebuked, than for Smyrna and Philadelphia, which are not.[16] This shows that Jesus understands that grace motivates and encourages those who are struggling to tackle what is amiss.

> 'Jesus understands that grace motivates and encourages those who are struggling to tackle what is amiss.'

The list of things acknowledged and praised about the church in Thyatira is also impressive. Christ said, 'I know your deeds, your love and faith, your service and perseverance, and that you are now doing more than you did at first' (Revelation 2:19). There was much to commend at Thyatira. Nevertheless, there was internal danger of the same kind as that in Pergamum (2:14) but it went even deeper.[17] The church tolerated 'that woman Jezebel, who calls herself a prophet. By her teaching she misleads my servants into sexual immorality and the eating of food sacrificed to idols' (2:20). Their tolerance of the wickedness which Jezebel signifies defiled the servants of Christ and seduced them into immoral conduct.

Again, praising and acknowledging the good in these churches did not prevent Christ from rebuking and warning them and instructing them to take the appropriate actions to remedy the situation. Since Christ appreciates what they have done for his sake before his rebuke, he communicates hope and the continuation of his love to them. The churches, then, when their weaknesses and wrongs are revealed, are not taken over by despair and hopelessness. Instead, they get encouragement from the strengths highlighted by Jesus and become hopeful of turning things around.

Jesus also used gratitude to encourage and strengthen the churches that were already doing well despite their difficult circumstances. The church of Smyrna was one of them. Christ acknowledged the fact that this church was going through various kinds of affliction and poverty. However, its poverty was only external. When talking about the inner life and spiritual strength of the church, Christ said that it was 'rich' (Revelation 2:9). The letter to Philadelphia also resembles that to Smyrna in that it is characterised exclusively by praise.[18] The church required neither reproach nor a summons to repent, but rather encouragement and support in the conflict with the Jews. The church remained faithful to the word of Jesus and had not denied his name, despite opposition.

Instrument of *shalom* in Jeremiah

- The Israelites show gratitude, not just through thanking God for his gifts, but by obeying his commands, even when it's hard.
- Jeremiah tells the Jews to pray for God's blessing on the people who have taken them into captivity.
- Living out gratitude like this, in obedience to Christ, allows us to become instruments of *shalom*, blessing and peace.

In the Old Testament, gratitude is exemplified through Israel's relationship with Yahweh. They are given the task of proclaiming his praises, goodness and character to the world as a kingdom of priests and a holy nation (Exodus 19:6). Among their priestly duties is the essential act of praising, worshipping and recognising Yahweh's blessings, guiding others to do the same. As a kingdom of priests and a holy nation, they're not only expected to verbalise their gratitude but also to live according to his decrees, reflecting his attributes in their lives and interactions (19:5). This not only brings glory to Yahweh but also inspires others to join in praising him.

Simply singing about his kindness and faithfulness isn't enough; it's the combination of worship with obedience that truly makes them a chosen people for Yahweh, distinct from the rest of the world. Gratitude, therefore, encompasses faithful obedience, and

Israel's role as a priestly kingdom and holy nation underscores how obeying God's commands is the ultimate expression of gratitude to Yahweh.

> 'Obeying God's commands is the ultimate expression of gratitude to Yahweh.'

Living a life of gratitude to God by obeying his instructions and by showing love and forgiveness to others, even to their enemies, was also a challenge that the Israelites had to face as a community. At times, they were faced with showing gratitude not as a response to kindness received, but as a gift offered. This had the potential to challenge and change their own human response to evil as well as changing the dynamics of their relationship with those who wronged them. In the process, it would make a way for God's purpose to be fulfilled.

Jeremiah 29 is an example of this. The exiled Jews were in a difficult situation. They were struggling to understand what had happened to their country, their people and themselves. They were trying to reconcile the promises of Yahweh with their ordeal. During loss, suffering and confusion, the Israelites were confronted with two voices. The first one was from the false prophets (Jeremiah 29:8–9), reminding them of the suffering the Babylonians had caused. This exacerbated their hatred and resentment, and drew a picture of a God who shared their anger and resentment and who would soon come to take vengeance on their behalf.

The second voice was from the prophet Jeremiah, commanding them to pray specifically for peace, *shalom*, for the all-encompassing blessing of Babylon. In other words, to wish, work and pray for the prosperity of the land of their enemy, since their prosperity depended on it: 'Also, seek the peace and prosperity of the city to which I have carried you into exile. Pray to the LORD for it, because if it prospers, you too will prosper' (Jeremiah 29:7).

In doing so, they were not only giving to the Babylonians that which they did not deserve, but they were also glorifying, introducing and imitating the God who gives, forgives and loves the unworthy and the undeserving. It is not hard to imagine the angry responses to such words among the captives, of course. Indeed, Psalm 137 shows us the depth of the anger and ugliness of the mood of the exiles on first arriving in Babylon, with their longing to go back to Israel and a desire for vengeance on their enemy.

For the exiles, praying and seeking the welfare of Babylon must have seemed impossible theologically, emotionally and politically. Despite the potential aggravation it would cause among the listeners in Babylon, Jeremiah insisted that this was the will of Yahweh for them. Once they could accept the perspective and the advice stated in verses 4–6 and had settled down as residents in Babylon, 'then they had an ongoing mission there'.[19] Their mission, Revd Dr Chris Wright asserts, was to be the continuation and fulfilment of Abraham's mission as a role model and source of blessing to all the nations. Like him, they would find that it 'turns mourners into missionaries'.[20] The outworking of their mission, therefore, involved seeking the *shalom* of their Babylonian neighbours, caring for their welfare and being agents of constructive peace and well-being in the communities in which they settled. This sacrificial act towards their enemies is a reminder of the words of Jesus to those who were under Roman occupation. Jesus said to them, 'I tell you, love your enemies and pray for those who persecute you' (Matthew 5:44).[21]

This sacrificial act, responding with good to those who did evil, had the potential to transform their relationship with the Babylonians. Gratitude here was expressed to God by obeying his commands concerning the Babylonians as a spark to start the gratitude dynamics which were potentially able to transform their relationships.

Gratitude in the nature and language of the Trinity

- Gratitude is at the heart of the way God the Father, God the Son and God the Holy Spirit relate to and communicate with each other.
- This has implications for us – we too should use the language of appreciation, gratitude, praise, joy and thanksgiving.

The Christian understanding of gratitude, similar to the other characteristics of Christian conduct, springs from the nature and the language of the triune God. The language and grammar expressed in the communion of the persons of the Trinity reveal how gratitude and appreciation both characterise the words one person of the Trinity uses to refer to another and shape conversation between them.

Jesus reveals his intimate relationship with his Father in a prayer charged with joy and thanksgiving (Luke 10:21-22). Whenever he communicates with him, he starts by praising and acknowledging who he is. He lives and dies to glorify his Father by obeying him and fulfilling his will.[22] In John 17, it becomes evident that, from Jesus' perspective, the glorification of the Son is not an ultimate goal in itself. Rather, it serves a greater purpose. Jesus embraces the cross, fully aware that through his sacrifice, he brings glory to his Father. This passage underscores that Jesus' ministry was never about seeking honour or recognition for himself. Throughout his mission on earth, he consistently and graciously pointed to the Father, highlighting that all his actions and teachings were meant to reflect the Father's glory and not his own.

The Father also uses a language of appreciation and gratitude when he speaks about the Son. His public declaration stands as testament to this fact. 'This is my Son, whom I love, with him I am well pleased' (Matthew 3:17). This message is conveyed from the heart of a satisfied Father. God's testimony is directed to the audience present. No explanation is necessary as to why this appreciation is given, since gratitude and appreciation are an overflow of the loving communion within the persons of the Trinity and a warm approval of the Son's role on earth.[23] God's purpose is that all should honour the Son even as they honour the Father (John 5:23). The Son is also addressed with a language of love and appreciation at the Mount of Transfiguration. In response to Peter's unwise words, the Father speaks, commanding those present, 'This is my Son, whom I love; with him I am well pleased. Listen to him!' (Matthew 17:4–6). This response indicates warm approval and that the Son's credentials are unrivalled.[24]

The Spirit also comes to reveal and glorify the Son. It is the Spirit who has his principal mission as the glorifying of Jesus.[25] He is the one who gives the knowledge and the ability to believers to know and confess that Jesus is Lord: 'no one can say, "Jesus is Lord," except by the Holy Spirit' (1 Corinthians 12:3). Speaking to his disciples about his departure, Jesus promises that he will send the Holy Spirit to be with them in his place. Explaining what the Holy Spirit will be doing when he comes, Jesus says, 'He will glorify me because it is from me that he will receive what he will make known to you' (John 16:14). The Spirit works to bring home the glory of Christ to the world.[26] In other words, the ultimate criteria for the Spirit's activity is the exaltation of Jesus as Lord. There is this language of glorifying one another and presenting the other to be greater. Jesus tells his disciples, 'it is for your good that I am going away. Unless I go away, the Advocate will not come to you' (John 16:7). In saying this, Jesus implies, among other things, the fact that the coming of the Holy Spirit is just as important as his own presence with them has been.

It is into this kind of communion and reciprocity that Jesus invited his disciples. Christ is not just an external example of Christian living. In the sacraments, Christians are joined to Christ in the power of the Spirit and participate in Christ's trinitarian pattern of life. The relations between the Father, the Son and the Spirit become the grammar of Christian conversation as well as a form of Christian living.[27]

Likewise, the pattern of the liturgy reveals the trinitarian dynamics of Christian living: everything comes from God the Father, through Christ, in the Spirit, and everything returns to God the Father, through Christ, in the Spirit (Ephesians 1:3–14).[28] Thus, it is participation in the humanity of Christ through the Spirit which enables believers to live a life of gratitude, both to the triune God and to each other. No one person of the Trinity is convinced that he is owed something or that the 'others' are less than he is.

The ecclesiastical necessity of gratitude

- Gratitude plays a vital role in creating churches that reflect God's love and priorities.
- To benefit from the different members of the body, we must adopt an attitude of gratitude, recognising and acknowledging our reliance on them. This means appreciating the unique functions each part performs, understanding how they contribute to the overall edification of the body.
- Where there is gratitude, Christians can benefit one another by appreciating each other's unique gifts.

Theological understanding of the nature and function of the Church also illustrates the role gratitude plays in Christian living. This role is particularly evident in Paul's imagery of the Church as the 'body' in 1 Corinthians 12. Discussing the diversity of the Church alongside its unity, Paul uses the image of the body to illustrate his point.

The essence of the analogy in 1 Corinthians 12:15–20 communicates the need for diversity if there is to be a true body.[29]

A body is one thing and, at the same time, it has many parts or members. Diversity and not uniformity is essential for a healthy Church. This body analogy implies the interdependent nature of Christian life and the requirement to acknowledge and appreciate the benefit and contribution of others.[30]

The eye cannot say to the hand, 'I don't need you', and vice versa (1 Corinthians 12:21). On the contrary, parts of the body which seem to be weaker are indispensable, and those parts thought to be less honourable, people invest with greater honour. All members are necessary if there is to be a healthy body. For the body to function properly, Paul argues that the Corinthians need to experience a variety of Spirit manifestations within the gathering community and recognise the value of each other's gifts.[31]

Therefore, if the Corinthians want to benefit from the diverse gifts in the body, their attitude towards others in the community should change.[32] They should not take an elitist view of a particular gift, which allows them to despise others and divide the community. Their mutual interdependence as a body necessitates acknowledgement and appreciation of the gift of the other. Thus, presenting the image of the body, Paul wants to encourage the members of the community to live in unity, with mutual help and appreciation – with gratitude.

The eschatological reality of gratitude

- When Jesus comes again as King of his new kingdom, gratitude will be a central feature.
- God will recognise the faithfulness of those who follow him, even though their actions are only possible because of his grace.

Gratitude is also reflected in the eschaton – in the eternal kingdom of God. In the fully fledged manifestation of the kingdom of God, gratitude is the language uttered by all creation. Alongside the heavenly beings who are worshipping God for who he is and for his justice and salvation, those who are redeemed by the blood of the Lamb worship their Redeemer with utter gratitude. Surprisingly, however, gratitude is not only expressed by the redeemed to their Redeemer – the Redeemer also acknowledges, appreciates and celebrates those who are redeemed. Their faithfulness is acknowledged and rewarded.

In Revelation 5, the redemptive work of Jesus is magnified and its crucial role is highlighted. John, as a representative of all humanity, stands in despair after discovering that no one is found worthy to open and read the scroll, or to look at it (Revelation 5:4). The great relief comes when one of the elders points to the Lamb who was slain and who was granted the authority to take the scroll from the outstretched arm of the one on the throne. After that, thanksgiving, praise and worship are ascribed to him out of gratitude and adoration.

The new song, the hymn by the angels, the praise of the whole creation, the affirmative 'Amen' of the four living creatures, and the adoration of the elders spring out of infinite gratitude for the redemptive work of the Lamb. This 'worthy' declaration – 'Worthy is the Lamb' – is not given to Jesus after considering certain prerequisites, but follows from the fact that 'such an event demands grateful high valuation'.[33] The Lamb is not only praised and worshipped but granted authority to sit on the throne and to reign over the world. The 'new song' in Revelation 5:9–10 elaborates the underlying reasons why the Lamb is worthy to assume his eternal reign over the world. The Lamb proves worthy because by his sacrificial death he redeemed people for God from all nations and constituted the redeemed as a 'kingdom of priests'.[34] In other words, Christ is thoroughly praiseworthy because, by his death, he has saved people from every part of the world – every continent, every country, every region. He has done this that together they may serve him forever in his eternal kingdom.

Thus, in God's eternal kingdom, gratitude is given to God and the Lamb. But not only to God and the Lamb. The saints or believers – who appropriated the redemptive work of the Lamb and faithfully completed their race with endurance and courage in the face of tribulation – also receive gratitude. A good example of this is seen in Revelation 7, where the vision of the international multitude before the throne symbolises those who have endured and survived the great tribulation that precedes the last day. The acknowledgement that they are 'the ones who have come out of the great tribulation' and 'have washed their robes and made them white in the blood of the Lamb' (7:14) indicates an appreciation of their commitment and love to God. This appreciation is confirmed by the rewards and privileges given to them (7:15–17).

In the life of the 'overcomers', it is the grace of God which accomplishes all that is worthy of praise. Therefore, all the glory, gratitude and praise is due to him. However, their effort to appropriate his grace and live a life of obedience and love does not pass without recognition and appreciation from God.

This is also found in the gospel narratives where God's eternal kingdom is implied. In the parable of the talents in Matthew 25, Jesus affirms the fact that those who are faithful in using their talents and who bear fruit will be acknowledged and rewarded when the Son returns: 'Well done, good and faithful servant! You have been faithful with a few things; I will put you in charge of many things. Come and share your master's happiness!' (Matthew 25:21).

The wickedness of ingratitude

- Ingratitude has a devastating impact on our lives and on our relationship with God and with each other.

The biblical and theological foundation

- Ingratitude leads to rebellion, chronic self-centredness and an open door to other evil behaviour.

In the New Testament, ingratitude is included in the lists of immoral behaviours and character traits. It is a bedrock on which all kinds of wickedness can flourish. In Romans 1, Paul describes ingratitude as a refusal to acknowledge and recognise the Creator with the praise that is due to him and a refusal to recognise humans as God's creation. Human self-dependency can cause patterns that are destructive both to ourselves and our communities. Paul asserts that what can be known about God – in other words, our basic perception of God – is possible for all human beings and is available for all to see: 'God's invisible qualities – his eternal power and divine nature – have been clearly seen, being understood from what has been made' (1:20).[35] Therefore, humanity is without excuse. Despite these general revelations about the Creator, men and women refuse to recognise him and give him praise. This refusal to acknowledge the Creator indicates a false sense of self-sufficiency and choice of independence. These lead to a decision to live for ourselves, rather than for God and others, and a deliberate stifling of the truth which challenges that self-centredness.[36]

This rebelliousness against the truth led God to let us have our foolish ways. The more we refuse to be grateful and recognise his benefits, the more we become entangled in our selfish, self-destructive and self-absorbed ways. This ingratitude becomes a fertile soil for immorality to prosper. Refusing to be grateful to God then often also causes ingratitude to others, as we fail to recognise the image and character of God in them. Notice how most of the immorality described here demonstrates ingratitude to others:

> They have become filled with every kind of wickedness, evil, greed and depravity. They are full of envy, murder, strife, deceit and malice. They are gossips, slanderers, God-haters,

insolent, arrogant and boastful; they invent ways of doing evil; they disobey their parents; they have no understanding, no fidelity, no love, no mercy.
(Romans 1:29–31)

We see further lists of the consequences of ingratitude in 2 Timothy 3, resembling the list in Romans 1. Paul warns Timothy that he lives in the last days and is seeing the fulfilment of eschatological prophecies. As Paul describes the opponents in Ephesus whom Timothy faces, who act and live in a way contrary to the gospel, he tells Timothy that he should not lose heart. He must understand that he is living in the last days – the context within which the appearance of these people must be understood.[37] The theme of self-centredness permeates the nineteen immoral behaviours listed here:[38]

People will be lovers of themselves, lovers of money, boastful, proud, abusive, disobedient to their parents, ungrateful, unholy, without love, unforgiving, slanderous, without self-control, brutal, not lovers of the good, treacherous, rash, conceited, lovers of pleasure rather than lovers of God – having a form of godliness but denying its power. Have nothing to do with such people.
(2 Timothy 3:2–5)

Although ingratitude is listed as one of them, the rest of the list could easily apply to the consequences of ingratitude. For instance, people can be boastful and proud, demonstrating an assumed self-sufficiency which takes no account of God and others. Ingratitude naturally follows from this inflated opinion of self, causing us to scorn others, even God. Timothy is advised: 'Have nothing to do with such people.'

Similarly, while giving instructions to his followers to imitate God in their actions towards their enemies by loving, doing good

The biblical and theological foundation

and lending to them without expecting anything in return, Jesus categorises the ungrateful and the wicked as God's enemies towards whom he shows kindness (Luke 6:35).

The story of the ten lepers also provides insight into Jesus' view on gratitude as well as ingratitude (Luke 17:11–19). The conclusion of the narrative speaks to what Jesus was saying all along to his disciples, as well as to the Pharisees.[39] Both groups were given the immense privilege of hearing the word of salvation from the lips of the Saviour himself. However, the Pharisees in particular, representing the majority, failed to respond to the message of Jesus with acceptance and gratitude. As such, the message of the story is directed to all who listen to and read the text.

Among the ten lepers, only one gave a heartfelt response to the Saviour who healed him, and this thankful man was the Samaritan, the outsider. Jesus was surprised by the ingratitude of the nine lepers who failed to pause to express gratitude for what they received. It is probable that the other nine lepers were from Judea.[40] It is the attitude of entitlement or taking privileges for granted which hinders the heart of gratitude. Nothing more is seen in Scripture of the nine ungrateful lepers. Therefore, the lesson is to be more like the one and less like the nine.

As we have seen in this chapter, gratitude is deeply rooted in the biblical narrative, from the first moments of God's creation to the visions of the new heaven and the new earth. In the gospel itself, in the actions and attitude of our Lord Jesus Christ, in the writings of Paul, in messages of Jesus to the seven churches and in the *shalom* encouraged by Jeremiah, we see gratitude as a pivotal component, one that fosters peace and harmony.

6

Gratitude and social change

In the midst of a moving mission seminar held in the heart of central London, I found myself engrossed in an interview with a seasoned sixty-two-year-old missionary. Born in the UK to a family of African descent, his reflections on identity resonated deeply with the room. When asked about his sentiments regarding his sense of self, he hesitated momentarily before saying, 'I don't feel like I am accepted in Britain as a British person and when I go to Angola where my family came from, I don't feel like I belong there either. People see me as a foreigner. It has been a struggle for me for a long time. However, I am now seeing myself more as an African than British.'

Despite acknowledging his African heritage, there was an underlying desire to embrace his birth country as his primary affiliation. This poignant narrative of rootlessness is far from unique; it is an experience shared particularly among the second generation of migrant communities, born in Britain, yet struggling to claim it as home – unless endowed with wealth or talent granting them special access and privileges.

I recall another encounter – this time with a German expatriate who had lived in Britain for nine years and married a woman of Ghanaian descent born in the UK. He recounted how, invariably, when meeting new acquaintances, inquiries about origin were directed solely at his wife because of her skin colour.

The problem of rootlessness and being an outsider

The pervasive sense of rootlessness experienced by subsequent generations of immigrants is a societal concern that cannot be dismissed. It transcends the realm of personal identity, impacting the fabric of the United Kingdom and its harmony. Only those who have navigated the labyrinth of identity crisis comprehend its profound anguish, powerlessness and vulnerability. Rootlessness fosters a quest for belonging and renders people susceptible to seeking solace in unhealthy alliances. This vulnerability, stemming from a lack of rootedness, serves as fertile ground for the recruitment tactics of those peddling radical ideologies.

A conflicting dichotomy emerges where individuals, who are citizens, protest in a manner like that of foreigners. Words are articulated that are not normally used in the context of one's country. That is not to say that we wouldn't expect angry exchanges when protesting against an unfair policy or legislation that the government is applying in its domestic or foreign governance. That is what makes the UK democratic, and it's our right as citizens to do so. However, we don't make the country as a whole the target and express our wish for its harm. That is what I mean by 'protesting as a foreigner'. We object to a specific wrong as a citizen who sees that something in their country needs changing, rather than criticising the country as a whole as an outsider.

The rage and anger we frequently witness in the Western world stems not only from the immediate cause of our protest but also from the deep-seated frustration born of rootlessness. It is evident, therefore, that the more fragmented our society becomes and the more isolated our communities grow, the greater the risk of exploitation by those who have a malicious agenda against the nation, creating fertile ground for extreme views and ideologies to flourish.

Gratitude and social change

The unrestrained protests witnessed on our streets are not merely a reaction to specific policies but a collective outcry stemming from an existential void. This identity vacuum is exploited by extremist elements, further fracturing communities and causing concern to both the government and society.

Significant investments are being made in the UK to foster integration and cohesion, with legislative measures aimed at combating extremism.[1] Yet, these efforts, while commendable, fail to address the root cause – the pervasive sense of rootlessness corroding societal bonds. In essence, addressing the fundamental yearning for rootedness is imperative for forging a harmonious and resilient society.

> 'Addressing the fundamental yearning for rootedness is imperative for forging a harmonious and resilient society.'

Moreover, a lack of inclusive national celebrations exacerbates this feeling of rootlessness, hindering the development of a shared national identity. Most of the national celebrations we have in Britain are exclusive. The exclusivity is not intentional, but since national celebrations involve sharing a common history or experience, they are by nature exclusive of those who haven't been part of that history. And, of course, it is possible for people to make these celebrations theirs through time and experience.

That is not to say that Britain, like any other nation, shouldn't have its unique national celebrations – in fact, we might need more.[2] Rather, this current exclusivity misses a critical opportunity to foster inclusivity. Inclusive national celebrations are key to welcoming newcomers into society and helping them forge a sense of national identity. By celebrating with a shared sense of history and experience, we cultivate common ground. Without this, alienation persists, and people are left with their feelings of being an outsider – feelings which are transferred from one generation to another.

The power of grateful celebration

So, what are we going to do about it? I propose that, again, gratitude holds the unifying element. It prompts us to celebrate the good bestowed upon humanity before addressing the challenges that divide us. The very act of acknowledging and celebrating the good is simultaneously a critique and an assault on that which is corrupted and not contributing to human flourishing.

As an immigrant in the UK who is deeply concerned about societal divisions, I seek solutions by promoting the importance and primacy of acknowledging and celebrating the good. The absence of such celebrations gives opportunities for negative influences to grow. To paraphrase Aristotle, nature abhors a vacuum. When good is ignored, it is the good that is demoted, allowing injustice to increasingly shape our engagement with others. However, when good is acknowledged and promoted, it creates an opportunity for a unified and concerted effort to tackle the wrongs in our society.

> 'When good is ignored, it is the good that is demoted.'

Celebration is a powerful tool to communicate and internalise the value of what is being celebrated. As we see in the book of Leviticus, God commands his people to hold seven feasts.[3] These are grounded on his provision and intervention and communicate who God is, how he relates to his people and what he has done for them. As they celebrate those feasts, they are transmitting and communicating history and creating a shared experience with the upcoming generation based on what God has done for them. Therefore, their identity and unity as God's people goes from generation to generation.

Similarly, to achieve our goal of fostering community cohesion and integration in order to internalise, embrace and celebrate British values (such as belief in freedom, tolerance of others, accepting personal and social responsibility, respecting and upholding the rule of law), we need to find a cause for celebration that is inclusive, relatable and common. Doing so will help cultivate a harmonious community and instil a sense of nationhood in the life of every individual in Britain.

One cause for celebration could be the ethnic riches of Britain, recognising this as a unifying force and honouring the valuable contributions that diverse communities have made and continue to make to the nation's past, present and future. Inclusive and relatable celebrations could foster a sense of nationhood, change how people engage with each other and fuel positive contributions. They provide a context to address concerns about community cohesion, integration and the potential exploitation of divisions by extreme ideologies while promoting British values.

Reflecting God's heart

As Christians, celebrating ethnic diversity aligns with theological principles. Diversity is integral to the gospel, breaking down barriers and creating one family in Christ. The divide Jesus broke between the Jews and Gentiles is representative of all divides – whether they are cultural, racial or ethnic; whether they stem from differences in gender, class, age or any other societal distinction that divides us. This is the mystery of Christ, the inclusion of *all* nations into the family of God (Ephesians 3:6), the inclusion of 'every nation, tribe, people and language' (Revelation 7:9). Paul is saying diversity is part and parcel of the gospel. The vision of the diversity in heaven urges us to live that reality now.

> 'The vision of the diversity in heaven urges us to live that reality now.'

> After this I looked, and there before me was a great multitude that no one could count, from every nation, tribe, people and language, standing before the throne and before the Lamb. They

were wearing white robes and were holding palm branches in their hands. And they cried out in a loud voice: 'Salvation belongs to our God, who sits on the throne, and to the Lamb.' (Revelation 7:9–10)

Celebrating ethnic diversity as a problem-solving strategy

Celebrating ethnic diversity could potentially resolve many problems.

1 It will usher people into the feeling of nationhood. Whether they came to Britain yesterday or fifty years ago, they will feel valued, recognised and accepted.
2 The way we see and engage with each other will change since we cannot hate that which we celebrate.
3 A sense of being celebrated and valued will fuel positive contributions and unite the UK. It is difficult to contemplate separation when you are feeling celebrated and valued. When that happens, the reciprocal opportunity will be distinctive.
4 We will have less cause to worry about community cohesion or integration, as the celebration will make people gravitate from seclusion to inclusion. People will feel valued enough to take a step towards the other, creating shared values and experiences.

Celebrations help people develop the heart to consider the values and challenges of the nation to be their own. As a result, they are less easily manipulated by people who have extreme and harmful agendas against the UK.

Celebration as a vehicle for social change

The title of this book – *The Gratitude Way: Creating common ground in a divided world* – highlights a pressing issue prevalent in

British society. The disintegration of social cohesion will eventually lead to an environment where extreme ideologies (far left, far right, religious extremism and so on) can make inroads into wider culture. This social disintegration poses a significant threat to the life of the country. By causing pressure to build on governmental institutions, it can drive them to legislate in ways that are contrary to the foundational principles of British values – for example, human rights, a commitment to individual freedom, tolerance of others, accepting personal and social responsibility, respecting and upholding the rule of law.

Furthermore, it highlights, again, the problem of rootlessness. While not directly responsible for the emergence of extreme ideologies, rootlessness often serves to undermine efforts to push back against their hateful rhetoric. In response to this multifaceted challenge, we should make every effort to celebrate ethnic diversity alongside the promotion of British values. Bringing communities together in positivity and gratitude will create shared experiences that lead to a greater feeling of mutual belonging.

By recognising and embracing the richness, resilience and contributions of diverse ethnic communities, society can forge a path towards inclusivity and unity. Such an approach not only acknowledges the intrinsic worth of each cultural heritage but also reinforces the values that underpin British society, thus strengthening its resilience against the divisive influence of extreme ideologies. Ultimately, by creating a setting that values diversity and supports democratic principles, we can effectively and honestly address today's complex social challenges.

Sociology and social change

Sociology investigates the complex fabric of society, examining how people interact within various contexts and exploring the dynamics shaping specific groups or nations. While it often shines a light on societal issues and the potential for reversing harmful patterns, criticism has been directed towards sociology and psychology for their perceived focus on negativity, while overlooking the positive aspects of society. Within this critique lies a call to recognise the constructive and meaningful interactions that occur within sociocultural phenomena, such as expressions of gratitude and acts of altruism.

By broadening its perspective to encompass everyday social disparities, sociology can uncover the positive contributions embedded within social interactions. This recognition hinges upon observing the attitudes and emotions of individuals as they navigate cultural norms and go about their daily lives. The framework of investigation within sociology is diverse and subject to ongoing debate. Central to this discourse is the acknowledgement that how we frame investigations and perceive social phenomena greatly influences their outcomes.[4] Various scholars have proposed approaches over the years, with an emphasis on embracing everyday interactions and viewing society through a relational lens.

Pierpaolo Donati, an Italian sociologist, advocates for a relational approach to sociology, which prioritises the understanding of social phenomena through the lens of relationships.[5] According to Donati, relational sociology shows that both individuals and social institutions are fundamentally shaped by their relationships. He argues that all aspects of human and institutional life are influenced by these relational dynamics, inevitably creating a shared reality. In daily interactions, we create and reinforce meaning through what he calls 'symbols' (for example, words and gestures). These symbols help us understand our own social and cultural contexts. In this framework, expressions of gratitude are revealed to be more dynamic than many would think, causing reciprocal and equal exchanges that begin to dismantle traditional societal hierarchies.

Furthermore, relational sociology suggests that social interactions initiate greater levels of reflective thinking. Carefully considering our relationship to the world around us will lead to new understandings of the needs, rights and duties before us. This new understanding becomes the first step in seeing true change in behaviours and attitudes, hopefully fostering a lasting harmony between individuals and communities. Gratitude is, therefore, seen as central to social change, which is only possible through changing social relations. This approach views social problems as rooted in relational issues, suggesting that solutions will involve creating new ways of relating, such as fostering gratitude, rather than external interventions, such as policies. Donati notes that a new civil society emerges when new forms of personal and social reflection develop outside the usual market and state structures.

Appreciative Inquiry and social change

In our current societal framework, the concept of 'good' often finds itself overshadowed, relegated to the periphery of our collective consciousness. Instead, we find ourselves entangled in a ceaseless pursuit of problem-solving, ensnared by the gravitational pull of each issue as it arises. These issues, whether within our organisational structures or within societal fabric, frequently carry with them a weighty historical lineage, their roots intertwined with the complexities of the past.

Consequently, our attempts to unravel the causes and implement solutions are often blocked by a lack of consensus, hindered by the complex narratives that have shaped these problems over time. In order to break free from this cycle, it becomes imperative to shift our perspective towards a more positive paradigm. By affording primacy to the 'good', to those aspects of our endeavours that are functioning effectively, we create a more fertile ground from which to approach challenges. It is within this realm of positivity that the true potential for change lies.

Yet, paradoxically, it is precisely this aspect – the power of the 'good' – that remains largely overlooked amid our fervent attempts to address the 'bad'. Our conventional approach to engagement with the world often revolves around the identification and mitigation of wrongs, a reactive stance that perpetuates a cycle of conflict and incomplete resolution.

However, by redirecting our focus towards nurturing and amplifying the good, we not only cultivate a more resilient and empowered mindset but also equip ourselves with the tools necessary to confront and transcend the challenges that lie ahead. This approach to society's challenges finds resonance in a methodology known as 'Appreciative Inquiry'. Appreciative Inquiry emphasises the transformative potential of embracing a mindset of positivity and abundance.[6] Bob Stiller, Founder of Green Mountain Coffee Roasters, notes the value of this approach in his own organisation: 'Appreciative inquiry is a way of bringing people together and focusing them on the positive, building on what works, and you can use it anywhere.'[7]

Appreciative Inquiry challenges the traditional problem-solving approach in organisational management by emphasising a positive, strength-based perspective.[8] Unlike conventional methods that focus on identifying and fixing problems, Appreciative Inquiry seeks to uncover and amplify what is already working well within organisations. This shift in mindset acknowledges that problem-solving, while necessary, can be limited in its ability to inspire growth and innovation.

Imagine approaching organisational change not by dwelling on shortcomings, but by embracing strengths and opportunities. Those who advocate Appreciative Inquiry believe that by fostering a culture of appreciation and gratitude, organisations can tap into their full potential. The approach is grounded in the belief that positive emotions, such as gratitude, play a crucial role in driving meaningful change. At its core, Appreciative Inquiry encourages a shift from problem-solving to possibility-thinking. It promotes a deep exploration of what is right and successful within an organisation, community or group. By focusing on these strengths, Appreciative Inquiry aims to catalyse transformative growth and development.

The principles of Appreciative Inquiry, as articulated by its founders David Cooperrider and Suresh Srivastva, provide a framework for guiding this approach. In practical terms, Appreciative Inquiry follows a four-step process known as 'The 4Ds': Discovery, Dream, Design and Destiny.[9] This approach involves reflecting on past successes, envisioning an ideal future, designing concrete plans for change and committing to action. Throughout this process, leaders play a crucial role in fostering collaboration and empowering individuals to drive positive change.

Critics may argue that Appreciative Inquiry overlooks or dismisses existing problems. However, proponents of Appreciative Inquiry maintain that it does not ignore challenges but rather reframes them as opportunities for growth and transformation.[10] By focusing on what is working well and building upon strengths, Appreciative Inquiry creates a foundation for sustainable change and innovation.

Appreciative Inquiry and gratitude share a common goal: to inspire positive change by recognising and amplifying the best in people and organisations. By embracing these approaches, leaders can cultivate a culture of appreciation and possibility, driving meaningful progress and transformation.

Andy Frost spoke about gratitude at the Gratitude Initiative Summit in 2022. He shares his insights on the essence of gratitude, its significance and how to celebrate it.[11]

In conversation with Andy Frost, Director of Share Jesus International

I've been on a journey exploring what gratitude means. I used to think it was just about saying thank you. I remember a teacher at a school assembly once saying you should say thank you. So I was 'thank you, thank you, thank you' – for everything. 'Juice? Thank you ... Biscuit? Thank you.' Even now, I'm on the bus, 'Thank you, driver. Thank you. Thank you. Thank you.' I went for a meal last night with my kids and my daughter said to me, 'Dad, you say thank you a lot, don't you?' And I said, 'Thank you.'

But I've realised that gratitude is much more than saying thank you. I used to think that it was about counting our blessings. During the Covid-19 pandemic, I would take a moment to think about what we weren't able to do but, at the same time, I'd count my blessings. 'What are the good things that I *can* do? What could we be thankful for God for in this moment?' But I've discovered gratitude is beyond just counting our blessings.

The first thing I've discovered is this: gratitude requires you to slow down. We live in a hyperconnected world with our phones and our distractions and Netflix and busyness – and we can lose what it is to slow down and just be in the moment, to see what is all around. We lose the idea of actually hearing our heartbeat. If we don't slow down, we fail to notice the good that is all around us. You can't be truly grateful if you're always in a hurry.

The second thing I've discovered is that gratitude is about acknowledging the good. Every day, we're surrounded with these news stories – a war or some other horrendous situation happening in the world all around us. And if we keep watching this material online, we can become so focused on all the bad and evil and destructive things that we lose the sense that there are some good things as well.

We can't acknowledge things unless we notice them. And it has to be authentic. My wife is keen on writing to her MP. And she writes to the MP on various issues – she doesn't often see eye-to-eye with the local MP. And she writes her various complaints and issues and things she wants to challenge the MP on.

But at the height of Brexit, she was so aware that the Chamber had become toxic, she messaged the MP at 10.30 one night, saying, 'I'm a Christian, and I just want to say that with all that's happening right now in Parliament, I'm grateful for you and your public service, and I'm praying for you.' Normally, it takes months for her to hear back, but within twenty minutes, the MP had emailed back saying, 'Thank you so much. I needed to hear that.' Gratitude isn't about being passive; it's about looking for things that we can appreciate in other people. Gratitude is about acknowledging the good.

And the third thing is that gratitude helps you see the person behind the thing. My kids buy me various birthday presents. They were the first people ever to buy me flowers. They thought, 'Well, Mum likes them, so we're sure Dad will like them too.' And they bought me my first Peppa Pig book and I'm very thrilled at that. And they also bought me this hat, which says 'World's Best Dad'. I never wear it except in the house if the heating's off. But it's not about the gift; it's about the fact that they gave it to me. It's quite precious. After all, they gave it to me because they appreciate me and they wanted to say, 'Thank you, Dad, for who you are.'

Gratitude is more than just seeing the gift – it's seeing the giver behind the gift. And it works on a child–father relationship. It also works on a much bigger level. But every day when I breathe in and I breathe out, I say thank you to God for this gift of life that he has given me. Gratitude is about relationships. It's about being grateful for someone or something, but it might not just be about physical things but about being present, about their affection, about their encouragement, about their support.

And here's a challenging thing: even when there is somebody that I strongly disagree with on certain topics, even their worldview, there is still something that I can be grateful to that person for. Gratitude helps you see the person behind the thing.

We often have difficult conversations, don't we? In our families, in our businesses, in our churches, in our communities. Gratitude, I think, begins to help us see how we navigate these difficult conversations. These conversations can be explosive and challenging, and there are two ways we need to try to tackle a difficult conversation. The first thing is that we begin the conversation with an apology. It's an amazingly disarming tool. It builds a bridge when you say, 'I'm sorry. I messed up. I got that wrong. I want to change that.' (The challenge with an apology is you can only begin with an apology if you have been wronged.) The second tool is gratitude. And gratitude isn't about sweeping the issues under the carpet it's about working out how we frame these conversations.

I'm working right now on something called the Movement for Recovery in different places around the UK, and in London as well. In London, we're going to look at various missions that Sadiq Khan has put in place for how we rebuild post-Covid. They've got nine different missions. One is around mental health and well-being. That's the first one we're going to focus on. But one of them is around social cohesion. They want to work out how we can build better communities going forward. What does it look like to bring different people from society together to dream about what our place could be like going forwards?

I think the Covid pandemic has shown us just how unequal society is on so many levels. We've all lived through the same pandemic. We've had very different experiences. For some of us, we have more savings in our banks, but some of us have been saved by food banks. There's that challenge and that divide that has become so visible. I met with the department on Zoom (as everyone did during that season). And I showed them the video of what happened in Islington – Girma's gratitude meal – where different people from Islington came together, were thanked, talked about gratitude and began these robust conversations about the future of the borough. And as they watched this video, they were amazed by it. Because they had lots of ideas and lots of teaching, lots of research was done, but this was a really practical model of what could happen in a community when you start the conversation with gratitude, bringing different people together.

So why do I support the Gratitude Initiative? It's because I want our communities to thrive. And where we start difficult conversations is important. For me, gratitude is an act of humility. Gratitude cuts through barriers. Gratitude creates a deeper human connection. Gratitude disarms aggressors. Gratitude can bring about reconciliation.

The what and the why – and finally the how.

How are we going to celebrate gratitude? I think, first of all, we need to celebrate gratitude *in the stories that we tell*. As soon as you hear the words, 'At the beginning...' or 'Once upon a time...' or 'In a galaxy far, far away...' you know a story is about to be told and you begin to get a little bit excited.

Because stories are powerful.

Stories help us to frame what is going on. Whenever I see my local Co-op and it's got a police cordon outside, I always wonder, 'What happened there? What is the story? What took place?'

Stories inspire. They get beneath our skin. They engage our emotions. When you watch adverts, you see how they play with our emotions. They do nice family ideas or nice emotional moments to try to retell a story to connect on a much deeper level.

And stories guide, helping us to know how we can live our lives differently. What are the stories that *we* have that we need to highlight and celebrate to demonstrate the power of gratitude? These stories can be contagious.

Another way we can celebrate gratitude is by *creating habits of gratitude*.

Culture is a really powerful thing. There's that saying that culture eats vision for breakfast. We can have this vision of gratitude, but how do we embed it in the way that we do things, in our habits? Habits form our culture – shared habits. And a habit is three things. It is a cue, an action and a reward. So, a very simple one – think of when we meet someone new: the cue is you meet someone new, the action is to put out your hand and do a handshake, and the reward is you've made that sense of connection with that person. The cue, the action, the reward.

I think we need to work out how we can create some habits around gratitude, perhaps in our workplace, perhaps in our church, perhaps in our community. Here's just one example.

The cue is this: you're going to a difficult meeting and you know it's going to be challenging. The action is to first pause, reflect, think about the good in the other person and open the meeting with a moment of gratitude. And I think the reward is this: we'll find that meetings go much better.

What are the stories we can tell? What are the habits we can create?

Finally, I think of the life of Jesus. He showed us how to live a life of gratitude. And he had some difficult conversations at times in his ministry.

The challenging thing is, how do we make this a part of our lives every day, living out a sense of gratitude? More than just saying thank you, it's about how we do life.

7

The benefits of gratitude

Mark is usually shy when it comes to public speaking. This time, it is different. He feels he has a lot to say about the subject matter. The opportunity is also attractive to him. It is typical for someone in his position to get the chance to speak to thought leaders in the city. The usual overwhelming and distracting self-consciousness is replaced by excitement about the nature of his talk.

He starts his talk with a question.

What if we stop the habit of waiting for a funeral to talk about a person's value and contribution?

At funerals, families, friends and attendees generally come with a mindset to reflect on the strengths of the person who has died – all the positive contributions they made during their life, what they meant to us. It is not that we forget their weaknesses or the wrongs they did, but we choose to see them through the lens of their goodness.

We may choose to do that because we know that blaming the dead is meaningless and that it is honourable and respectful to say good things about them. After all, the dead don't get the opportunity to prove us wrong. On the other hand, it may be because death forces us to pause from the activity of life to see things from a broader perspective, reminding us of our mortality. Or maybe we're generous in what we think and say because we hope people will do the same for us when our turn comes.

It is not only death that gives us an opportunity to focus in on the strength, beauty and value of others. Life-threatening sickness, going far away from our family, city or country could do the same. It soon becomes apparent how much the people around us (or far away from us) mean to us. We start to regret missed opportunities, not spending ample time with them, thinking of the things we should have said when we had a chance.

And this is true not only of people, but also of our surroundings and all the good in our life. At particular moments, we realise how our busyness robs us of the opportunity of enjoying, appreciating and living life to the full. Unfortunately, this usually occurs when we encounter the possibility of loss. Once we realise the value of those around us, all that life has brought to us, we stop looking at them as a means or an instrument to an end that never seems to take us to a place of fulfilment.

Mark pauses for a few seconds and looks at the faces of the people in the room, then continues his talk.

For me, it took the death of my younger sister to wake me up to a life of wonder. To wake me up to the richness and beauty of people, places and all that is at my disposal. My sister was the unique one in our family. She had grounding mindfulness which none of us had. She would sit with strangers, young and old, listening to their stories and asking questions and end up building longstanding relationships with them. She had the ability to invoke the good in others. There was no dull moment with her; life was full of wonder, excitement and goodness. She had a lot to say about the mundane things of life. And she cultivated this even deeper consciousness of the moment after a car accident which made her wheelchair dependent.

She became very appreciative of the little things she could do and access. There were times when she acted as if she'd seen

The benefits of gratitude

something for the first time – the trees nearby, the view from the bridge which she had walked on for years or the colourful Sunday market that had been going on for years. It was as if she'd never considered them worthy of her time and attention before. Her appreciation and gratitude for the little things in life became contagious.

Although I appreciated her changed posture in life, her thoughtfulness and depth, I never understood it enough to want to imitate her. After her passing, I experienced lots of emotions. At times, I felt guilty for not spending enough time with her, angry at her death at a young age, and sad for not having her around. Since her death, I've met many people who said a lot of good things about my sister that were thought-provoking.

As I contemplated the final five years of my sister's life, after her accident, I began to grasp what she was saying about how her appreciation of the little things in life opened her eyes to see the beauty and gift of life. How it introduced her to a life of wonder instead of living in an attitude of assumption. As I put into practice my sister's posture in life, I progressed and became a thankful observer which improved my awareness, communication, relationship and worldview. It wasn't an easy journey to give up my obsession with dealing with life primarily from a problem-oriented approach and swap it for a recognition of the good as a starting point for viewing life. Over time and with intentionality, I developed a habit of gratitude that led me to see beyond the surface and a calmness that brought depth to my reflection and made me engage with difficult situations from a place of hope instead of despair.

Mark concludes his talk by opening the floor to questions. He begins answering them, visibly surprised by the number of hands raised.

Gratitude gives depth to our thinking

The renowned German philosopher Martin Heidegger undertook an extensive exploration of the intricate relationship between the acts of 'thinking' and 'thanking'.[1] He noted a profound connection between gratitude and our perception of existence, arguing that cultivating a sense of thankfulness and appreciation leads to a deeper understanding of our being in the world.

Heidegger famously stated, 'Thinking ought not to be confined solely to scientific or philosophical inquiry but should encompass a profound contemplation of the essence of existence within the world, a contemplation inherently intertwined with gratitude.'[2] His observation that deep reflection is connected with gratitude underlines gratitude's transformative power. It suggests that gratitude possesses the capacity to engender a heightened awareness, drawing us closer to an authentic understanding of the natural order of things.

While Heidegger's analysis primarily explores existential and philosophical dimensions, it also alludes to the theological implications of gratitude. This suggests that gratitude imparts ontological significance to reason, enhancing our awareness of existence in all its complexity. Gratitude, in this context, endows our perception of reality, truth and goodness with value, emphasising the intrinsic worth of the natural world and human existence beyond mere functional purposes.

In thinking about Heidegger's insights, it becomes evident that gratitude serves as a lens through which we can perceive the world, enabling us to look at humanity and the entirety of reality in its unadulterated truth, rather than viewing them solely as a means to an end. His critique extends to post-Enlightenment rationalism, which, he contends, has severed human understanding from the innate quest for divine truth, reducing the world to a realm of mechanised activity.

The benefits of gratitude

Adopting an attitude of gratitude invites a profound shift in perspective, leading us to recognise and appreciate the inherent goodness of our surroundings. This does not negate the existence of injustices or adversities but argues for a transformative approach to addressing them. Echoing the sentiments of the Danish philosopher Søren Kierkegaard, gratitude transcends mere rational assessments of the world's orderliness or fairness. Instead, it serves as a framework for interpretation – a guiding framework rooted in love – that shapes our interpretation of existence and imbues it with profound meaning and significance.[3]

Heidegger and Kierkegaard both assert that gratitude is a fundamental disposition that deepens our understanding of reality, imbuing it with compassion and emotional integrity. Through gratitude, we engage in a process of discovery, wherein the inherent goodness of the world becomes increasingly evident, providing solace and inspiration amid life's challenges and uncertainties.

Gratitude informs our discipleship

The concept of gratitude profoundly shapes our journey of discipleship, as is particularly evident in the narratives of the New Testament. Within its pages, gratitude emerges not merely as a fleeting emotion, but as a foundational disposition displayed in those touched by grace and called to walk the path of Christ. At the heart of the new covenant lies a stark acknowledgement of humanity's brokenness and imminent judgement, contrasted with the profound message of redemption brought forth by Jesus Christ.

Central to this narrative is the sacrificial act of Jesus, who willingly laid down his life for the salvation of sinners, a demonstration of unparalleled love and grace. Likewise, the Father's willingness to offer his Son for the sake of humanity underscores the depth of divine love and mercy. This narrative becomes a beacon, drawing believers into a perpetual state of gratitude towards God and their fellow humans. The ongoing remembrance of the transformative gifts given through the new covenant amplifies the depth of gratitude within believers. Through this covenant, individuals are granted salvation and welcomed into the collective body of Christ, where they find fellowship, edification and a shared mission of reconciliation.

These facets of the Christian journey serve as continuous wellsprings of gratitude towards God, fellow believers and humanity at large. Gratitude thus assumes a pivotal role as a framework of interpretation, as a method to find out the meaning behind words or behind life as a whole, as God intended it to be seen and understood. It instils a perspective that discerns the inherent giftedness of life and recognises God's active and benevolent presence in the world, unveiling his plan of salvation. This transformative outlook culminates in a lifestyle reminiscent of the Eucharist, fostering a habitual attitude of gratitude that permeates every aspect of a disciple's existence.

In his epistle to the Philippians, the apostle Paul exhorts believers to emulate the attitude of Christ, both in their relationship with God and in their interactions with others. This call to adopt a Christ-like disposition underscores the intrinsic connection between gratitude and the imitation of Christ. It entails humility, selflessness and a genuine appreciation for the qualities of others – a holistic embodiment of gratitude in action. Paul further emphasises the significance of intentional thought patterns in nurturing an attitude of gratitude. In Philippians 4:8, he urges believers to dwell on thoughts that align with the character of Christ, promoting a mindset characterised by truth, virtue and praise.

This deliberate cognitive shift serves as a safeguard against negativity and fosters a disposition of gratitude even in challenging circumstances. Similarly, in his correspondence with the Thessalonian church, Paul underscores the imperative of gratitude amid adversity. Despite facing persecution and affliction, believers are called to maintain an attitude of thanksgiving as an expression of their newfound relationship with God through Christ. This command, rooted in divine authority, reaffirms the Christian identity and the unwavering hope found in Christ, even in the midst of trials. Ultimately, the practice of continual thanksgiving emanates from a profound awareness of God's sovereignty and providence. It transcends mere appreciation for blessings and extends to a comprehensive worldview shaped by the redemptive work of Christ. Through this lens, believers navigate life's complexities with unwavering gratitude, acknowledging God's ultimate purposes and trusting in his overarching plan of redemption.

Gratitude helps us embrace lament

Gratitude, with its profound depth and expansive reach, emerges as a formidable force capable of reshaping our perception of the world, inviting us to delve into the murky depths of lament with a newfound sense of purpose and resilience. Much like the miraculous emergence of life from obscurity – the seed breaking through the soil, the unborn child flourishing within the womb, or the Saviour triumphantly emerging from the tomb – gratitude too springs forth from the shadows of sorrow, refusing to yield to the oppressive weight of adversity that seeks to overshadow our existence.

The resounding words of Isaiah 61:3 echo through the corridors of time. In this divine exchange, mourning is transformed into joy, ashes into beauty, and despair into praise, fashioning us into towering oaks of righteousness, testaments to the unmatched splendour of the Almighty. They serve as a poignant reminder of divine promises that transcend the realm of despair and suffering. Gratitude, therefore, emerges as a defiant anthem amid the sober symphony of lament, boldly proclaiming that evil shall not reign supreme, nor shall it dictate the course of our narrative.

The benefits of gratitude

Lament, spoken in the sacred language of covenant relationship, initiates its plaintive cry by extolling the virtues of a steadfast and unwavering God – whose character is defined by unyielding faithfulness and boundless compassion. It is a solemn acknowledgement of divine presence amid the tumultuous waves of suffering, a testament to God's unwavering solidarity with his afflicted children. Yet, lament does not languish in the depths of despair. Rather, it rises with a resolute affirmation of God's sovereignty, acknowledging his redemptive power to transmute suffering into triumph.

Amid the tapestry of hope, the resurrection of Christ emerges as a beacon of light, ushering in the comforting presence of the Holy Spirit – the divine Comforter. In the midst of lament, voices clamour in protest, denouncing the pervasive brokenness and injustice that mar the fabric of our world. However, gratitude refuses to remain a passive bystander; instead, it emerges from the crucible of suffering, acknowledging the divine presence in the agonising depths of human experience. Gratitude, as a defiant voice in lament, fosters a community of solidarity and compassion, offering a sanctuary for the expression of grief and pain.

It beckons the collective to draw near, to intimately empathise with the lamenting soul, and to actively engage in the pursuit of justice and reconciliation. For it is in our willingness to listen and to deeply identify with the suffering of others that we become co-labourers with God in effecting meaningful change within our world. Lament, arising as a fervent prayer of petition, stems from a profound awareness of the pervasive suffering and pain that plague our world. It stands as a sacred act of resistance – a bold proclamation against injustice and a fervent plea for transformation.

Yet, the absence of lament within our liturgical practices threatens to desensitise us to the suffering of others, impeding our ability to engage with genuine empathy and compassion. Gratitude, therefore, emerges as a steadfast companion in the tumultuous journey of lament, shining as a beacon of hope in the enveloping darkness. Its echoes resonate through the Psalms and the wisdom literature of ancient Israel, where praise and thanksgiving intertwine seamlessly with the cries of distress. Even in the direst of circumstances, gratitude remains a steadfast testament to the enduring faithfulness of God.

The timeless example of Job is a poignant reminder of this profound truth. Despite enduring unimaginable loss and unfathomable suffering, Job steadfastly refuses to relinquish his gratitude. His response to his wife's anguished counsel is a testament to his unwavering faith in the divine providence, affirming that even in the darkest of trials, God's love remains an unwavering constant. It is this steadfast conviction in the inherent goodness of God that enables Job to offer thanks in all circumstances, even during the most agonising moments of his existence.

Gratitude enhances our well-being

His concern for his wife Lola continued to grow by the day. She was given a long break from her work – not because she was explicit about her situation to her managers, but because they could see that she was not being productive and relationally conducive. Her anxiety and depression had started to surface. Before that, it was hard to differentiate her anxiety from her personality. She had a tendency to gravitate towards sad stories, incidents, tabloid headlines and things that happened a thousand miles away. She'd pick one negative or sad story and talk about it the whole day. The more she talked about it, the more she got saddened and all her attention would be swallowed by that particular story, making her unavailable for any other conversation or emotional engagement.

Her husband Darren stopped trying to show her the danger of exclusive consumption of the negative. He used to tell her, 'When you hear bad stories, of course feel sad about it. That's natural. Then ask

The benefits of gratitude

yourself if there is anything you can do to help. If there is, then do what you can; if not, move on. Remember, for every sad story, there is a good one too; talk about those stories as well.'

Lola never took his comments seriously or gave any attention to them. Now, he doesn't try to convince her – he deliberately refuses to engage in a conversation when she starts to talk about negative or sad stories. He was hopeful that his disengagement would help her to be conscious of her obsession with the negative.

Through time, her propensity for the negative started to affect their relationship. Any suggestion about finances or holidays was met with reasons and associated negative stories about why it would not work. She'd talk about the potential dangers and risks associated with the suggestion.

Her situation was now on another scale. She was anxious about everything, restless, melancholy and displayed emotional upheaval. Lola knew that what was happening to her was not normal – and the realisation made her even more anxious. The only constant in her life was her husband. For the first time ever, she told him how much she appreciated his support, availability, acceptance and consistency and decided to open up to him.

The opportunity came to her one Saturday morning when Darren was serving her breakfast in bed. That was when Lola opened up to him about all the things that were happening in her mind. Darren already knew everything. She didn't tell him anything that he wasn't aware of. It was her request for advice that surprised him. He saw that she was sincere. Once he was convinced that she was willing to listen to his advice and promised to follow it through, he got up and left the house, telling her that he would be back soon.

He went to the nearby supermarket and bought two pairs of sunglasses in different colours. He returned home and said to his wife, 'Look at these two pairs of glasses. One pair are the "glasses of negative perspective". The second pair are the "glasses of the wonders of life". You have been wearing one of these for a very long time – and

The benefits of gratitude

you know which ones. Now you will be wearing the glasses of wonder for the next six months and you will tell me what surprised you and what amazed you, and about the good you noticed. Whenever you start to talk about the negative, I will remind you about the glasses you are wearing.'

Lola agreed and started the journey of wonder.

Six months passed and Lola couldn't believe how the change from one pair of glasses to another had made such a difference in her mental and emotional life.

In the extensive landscape of psychological inquiry, a growing curiosity has emerged surrounding the profound impact of gratitude on human flourishing and overall well-being. Historically, the concept of gratitude has been largely overshadowed within the realms of psychological discourse, receiving minimal attention and recognition, indicative of its overlooked significance. Even within scholarly works such as the *Handbook of Cognition and Emotion* and the *Encyclopedia of Human Emotions*, discourse on gratitude is conspicuously sparse, reflecting a neglect of its intrinsic value.[4]

However, in recent decades, a paradigm shift has occurred as psychologists acknowledge and research the multifaceted nature of gratitude. This surge of interest can be attributed to various influential factors shaping contemporary psychological inquiry. First, the advent of positive psychology, spearheaded by luminaries such as Martin Seligman and Mihaly Csikszentmihalyi, has ushered in a newfound appreciation for positive emotions and virtues, with gratitude emerging as a focal point of exploration.[5]

Second, there has been a resurgence of attention among social scientists towards the religious and spiritual dimensions of human existence, recognising the pervasive presence of gratitude across diverse cultural and religious traditions. The resurgence of virtue ethics within the domain of moral philosophy has further

The benefits of gratitude

underscored the significance of gratitude as a virtue essential for cultivating moral character and fostering ethical conduct. The evolving understanding and conceptualisation of gratitude has thus mirrored these broader intellectual currents, emanating from a collective endeavour to observe, question and delineate the manifold benefits associated with the practice of gratitude in everyday life.

Psychologists, as devoted observers of the human psyche, have long recognised the asymmetrical impact of negative events and thoughts compared with their positive counterparts. This cognitive predisposition, explained by the tenets of Cognitive Behavioural Therapy (CBT), elucidates how the gravitational pull of negativity can ensnare us in a perpetual cycle of despair. Yet, amid this psychological landscape, gratitude offers a pathway to liberation from the controls of negativity. Cultivating gratitude involves embarking on a deliberate journey of inner transformation, where we consciously attune our mental faculties to perceive and appreciate the myriad blessings that grace our lives.

By directing our gaze towards the benevolent forces that surround us, we unlock the door to a realm filled with light and positivity, shielding us from the traps of despair and self-pity. In recognition of the profound psychological benefits of gratitude, in 2018 the Department of Psychology at the University of Sheffield, then under the visionary leadership of Dr Fuschia Sirois, embarked on a bold and ambitious endeavour. Their mission: to instil a culture of gratitude within the very heart of their community. Thus, the city became a canvas for their vision as they unveiled a monumental gratitude wall in its busy centre.[6]

A testament to the power of collective appreciation, this interactive monument invited locals to pause and reflect, to write down three heartfelt expressions of gratitude, thereby sowing the seeds of positivity amid the urban landscape. As the unveiling of the gratitude wall coincided with the grand spectacle of the

'Festival of the Mind', an event that celebrates mental health, Dr Sirois articulated the profound significance of their endeavour. Amid the noise of life's challenges, the gratitude wall stood as a supporter of resilience, encouraging individuals to embrace the radiance of positivity, thereby strengthening their mental fortitude and well-being.

Beyond its individual implications, gratitude transcends the limits of the self, weaving a tapestry of interconnectedness and reciprocity within the social fabric. In nurturing a spirit of gratitude, we foster bonds of compassion and altruism, forging pathways to mutual understanding and solidarity. Conversely, the branches of resentment, born from a negative experience, serve only to sow seeds of discord and estrangement, perpetuating cycles of bitterness and hostility. In the grand tapestry of human existence, gratitude emerges as a virtuous thread, weaving its way through the intricate interplay of individual and communal well-being. It is a testament to the resilience of the human spirit, a beacon of hope in the darkest of times. As we embark on the journey of life, let us heed the call of gratitude, for in its embrace lies the promise of well-being, transformation and transcendence.

Fuschia Sirois is Professor of Social and Health Psychology at Durham University. Her research explores gratitude within the broader context of identifying factors that contribute to risk or resilience in health and well-being outcomes.[7]

In conversation with Professor Fuschia Sirois

How do you define gratitude?
The definition that I go by when I research gratitude is the one that most people in psychology use, and it's comprised of

two main components. It's about being able to notice and then appreciate the positive in life. So, it's a very simple definition, but there's a lot packed within those ideas.

One of the key things we often think about is being thankful and appreciative. We see these types of feelings and words associated with gratitude, and certainly they are there. However, the necessary and critical first step, before you can be grateful, is to be able to notice the positive. It's one thing to say you can appreciate the positive, but if you don't see things around you as being positive, you don't notice small positive things in your life. That's going to make it very hard to experience some gratitude and to be grateful to others. It's something we often overlook. It's about noticing first and then appreciating.

What does research on gratitude tell us about gratitude?
My research is broadly defined as looking at the factors for risk and resilience for people's health and well-being. And gratitude is one of those factors.

One of the reasons I've studied gratitude in the context of chronic illness is because when you live with a chronic health condition or a chronic illness – such as something like heart disease or diabetes or arthritis or a variety of other conditions that people struggle with – it puts constant stress on you. And some of the early benefits that come out of gratitude are that it is beneficial for reducing stress.

Individuals who are in a situation where they experience ups and downs, due to their symptoms, may be experiencing pain, fatigue or limitations on the things they'd like to do. The findings coming out of our research were suggesting that people who were grateful in those conditions were faring much better than those who weren't experiencing gratitude.

When I say 'experiencing gratitude', I mean regularly. The way to look at gratitude is not just as a *state* – when someone does something nice for you, you thank them, and you have a state of gratitude. You have those nice, warm, positive feelings and you feel grateful.

But we also talk about having a *grateful mindset* or having a *grateful orientation*. And these are people who have just developed a way of dealing with life and looking at life that allows them to more easily and readily notice and appreciate the positive.

The research we undertook looked at these people who had this grateful mindset. In one of the first studies, we looked at two different chronic health conditions, arthritis and inflammatory bowel disease. And we found in both of those illness groups that individuals who had a more grateful mindset had lower levels of depression and better overall well-being six months later.

You might argue that there are lots of other factors that could contribute to depression and well-being and that it's not just about gratitude. So, we applied a very rigorous model that accounted for initial depression levels, other stressors, fatigue and illness-related variables. We threw pretty much everything into that model that we could. I remember at the time we were running the models, I thought, 'Oh, this is going to wipe out any effects of gratitude, because there are other factors that are explaining why we're seeing this association with gratitude and better well-being in these individuals who are struggling with their chronic health condition.'

And what amazed me was that nothing wiped out the effect of gratitude. It stood on its own, distinct from everything else, and was very powerful. The amount of what we call 'variance' or the amount that is explained in the outcomes was not huge, but it was stable. And when you're living with a chronic health condition, any little thing that can improve your well-being is valuable.

So that's one of the more remarkable studies we've done, I think. To me, it highlighted the power of gratitude and what it can do, especially for people who are under such stressful conditions.

Could we say gratitude helps us cope or even thrive in difficult circumstances?
If you're living day to day with stressors and uncertainty, there are certainly parallels with chronic illness. One of the factors that we know makes life stressful for people is not having a sense of control over things. When things are unpredictable, we feel stressed. When we also experience uncertainty, on top of not being able to control things, it makes it difficult to know where things are going. That describes people living with a chronic health condition in many instances, but it also describes many other difficult circumstances.

Therefore, I think there are very strong parallels between living with a chronic health condition and living in a difficult circumstance. In the same way, we have to be able to notice those small things that do make a difference. If we're focused on the negative all the time, on what's gone wrong, on the uncertainty and the anxiety, that takes up a lot of our energy and a lot of our focus, and there's no room left really to notice anything positive.

But if you're able to pull out even just a few positive things it can make a huge difference. Maybe some things that people have done for you, things that you've learned about yourself – perhaps by living under more difficult circumstances – or maybe you've grown closer in your relationships to others, just anything positive at all. And recognising those things, also just savouring them gratefully, I think can make a huge difference and reduce your stress.

We could describe it as 'coping', but it's more than that. A lot of the researchers on gratitude have said that it's not just coping. We and others have tried testing it. It's more than coping. Being grateful is an incredible phenomenon because it's not explained easily by coping and other things, but we know it has these beneficial effects. So, I think it's something that can be really valuable for people.

How do you think gratitude contributes to social harmony?
One of the things we know about gratitude is what we call 'social emotion'. We can certainly be grateful for things when we look around when we're alone, but we often experience gratitude in the presence of others – often for things that they might do for us. But we can also be inspired by other people's gratitude to be more grateful ourselves.

This is one of the things that came out of the event that Chris Blackmore and I pulled together a few years back, called the Sheffield Wall of Gratitude. We set up some cards with a classic gratitude exercise. It's a tool that you use to train yourself to be more grateful. And over time, you can develop more of this 'I'm grateful' mindset. It's called 'three good things'. You write down three good things in your life, or things that happened to you today.

We left it wide open for people to do. We had these cards available in different languages as well, so that it could be more inclusive that way. And we laid the cards out on the table and we had a huge wall – it was a massive wall in Sheffield's Millennium Gallery.[8] And we had taped-off spaces for what we called 'gratitude bricks'. And the idea was that there are so many walls being put up *between* people, why not put up a wall of gratitude to bring people *together* – the antithesis of that!

Even before the end of the first day, the wall was full. We had to start curating and taking things down to make space for other people so they could put their three things up because every new group of individuals that came in would do the same thing. They'd read – and now there were hundreds of these things up there – and they were like, 'Oh, I want to do this too.'

In terms of social harmony, I think that when we see or hear about what other people are grateful for, it reminds us to be grateful. And grateful not just for things, but for people. And in that way, it can create social harmony. When things are difficult and someone does something for us, it means that much more. Expressing that gratitude or hearing about other people who are grateful has that contagious element to it that can bring people together in a very powerful way.

How do we cultivate an attitude of gratitude?
Several of us researchers have been trying out a number of different techniques and methods in experimental studies over the last couple of decades. There are two that seem to be the most effective. One of them is similar to what we did with

the wall of gratitude, which is just simply writing down three good things. It's just a list, like a gratitude list. Usually at the end of the day, you would just sort of contemplate what three good things happened to you.

The format that takes can vary. We did this with the Sheffield Wall of Gratitude. They could download the lists as well, and they could take bricks home with them and do it. But also – and this is something I've done with my family – you can do this exercise around the family dinner table, right? It brings in that social element. Or it can be a private thing that you do for yourself. Or you can just take turns: 'OK, what are your three good things today?' And that way you learn about what's going on in the lives of your friends and family members and, at the same time, you're learning to cultivate that grateful mindset.

There's evidence to suggest this is best done at the end of the day. So, if you're doing it on your own and not in a family context like I just described, doing it just before you go to bed has been proven to improve your sleep and your sleep quality. People sleep better when they write down the things that they're grateful for. It has a very powerful effect, because you're ending your day not worrying about all the things you didn't get done and all the things that didn't go right. You're thinking about the things that went pretty well and that you're grateful for. And that allows you to sort of relax a bit more and enjoy a better night's sleep.

The other technique is similar, and it's something that you might do daily or more spontaneously, and it's what we call a gratitude diary. There are a lot of apps out there now as well. And there are apps also for those three good things. You can go onto your phone and look at the App Store or Google Play

The benefits of gratitude

Store. If you search for 'gratitude', a whole bunch of different ones will come up.

There are lots of ways to support the effort to cultivate a gratitude mindset. You can have a paper gratitude diary, or an electronic one – some of them allow you to put in pictures, or just write it like a diary. It's not as formalised as three good things, but it's the same kind of idea.

Conclusion

John Barnes, in his book *The Uncomfortable Truth about Racism*, concludes that changing laws or legislating new ones won't, on its own, bring a societal change in the way we see and treat each other.[1] He writes, 'If we want to strive for equality, it is extremely important to expose the lies that have historically been told about disenfranchised and marginalised groups.' He demonstrates these facts by giving an example of the limitations of the existing laws in bringing the desired changes in society. He says that what needs to change are the deep-rooted perceptions that have been ingrained in us through time. 'This is the reason why I say laws alone can't truly change things, as was demonstrated back then. The only way for meaningful change [in society] is to change perceptions before laws.'[2]

As to the question of how we should go about re-conditioning our minds and perceptions, among other things he suggests 'constant continued influences and debate, subliminally and implicitly', and the need for empathy with the perpetrators, understanding that they are victims of a system that indoctrinated them. However, Barnes appreciates the difficulties people have with engaging in honest and meaningful conversations about issues for fear of being criticised and he encourages them to be bold and courageous.

He is spot on in both his diagnosis and his prescriptions for the remedy of society's relational transformation, as he sees it – how a shift in our perception is the key to changing the way we see and relate to each other. However, he does not provide a solution for the difficulties people have in coming forward to engage in honest conversation, something that could create opportunities to encounter wrong perceptions. In dealing with difficult issues which have historical and contemporary baggage, the atmosphere in which the discussion is conducted is of paramount importance. It is this ability to create a conducive atmosphere in the hearts of the people involved, as well as in the room where the discussion is conducted, that makes gratitude unique and effective.

A uniquely effective solution

The favourable environment that gratitude creates is helpful for the perpetrators, as it takes away threatening aspects of the conversation and encourages them to take a listening posture without being defensive. But it also helps the victims. In the process of addressing evil or wrongdoing, we may still be affected by its influence, leading us to hold on to or operate from feelings of resentment, bitterness or anger. This can be disempowering, prohibiting us from articulating the issues clearly and impairing the desired outcome.

However, when we start by acknowledging the good, no matter how small the good in that situation is, we will become free from the influence of evil. As such, gratitude creates a framework for authentic conversation. And it creates a favourable atmosphere for a constructive conversation, where a change of not only perception but also language occurs, leading to a change of relationship.

It means that in our dealings with others, and the world as a whole, we will begin by acknowledging the good, noticing the good and talking about the good. Our criticism of the world only makes sense if we intentionally give primacy to the good in the way we see the world. It follows, then, that dealing with the bad and the evil should start by acknowledging the good. The good is the motivation to deal with the bad. The good is the overarching climate within which the bad is dealt with.

Gratitude also informs us that if what we want is a genuine and authentic change of the wrong, we must take human psychology and our fallen nature into account. Because of these two things, no matter how wrong we are, we don't respond positively to accusation, condemnation or confrontation. When confronted, challenged or condemned, we enter into a survival mode, 'fight or flight'. Either we fight, becoming defensive and hostile, or we give lip service and avoid further conversations altogether. When we put people in a survival mode, we may feel a release or a relief of our pain, because we have said what was on our minds and even made the other person feel guilty. We are, however, unlikely to experience true repentance when acting out of condemnation. Condemnation robs those we confront of the hope for forgiveness and restoration, even if they might have been open to repentance.

Gratitude as a worldview: its benefits

Considering gratitude as a worldview and recognising its definition as an acknowledgement of the primacy of the good has many implications.

Gratitude doesn't condone evil but facilitates dealing with it from a different angle, creating the impetus for lasting change.

Gratitude is a solution-oriented approach to resolving conflict.

Gratitude speaks the truth in love. It functions from the concept that we overcome evil with good.

Gratitude is the restorative arm of justice. Justice deals with the ideal, enforcing the full extent of the law. Gratitude, while endorsing the enforcement of the full extent of the law, recognises that we are all short of the ideal, and as such deserve a second chance.

Gratitude highlights how our manner in pursuing justice is as important as the justice itself and makes both the manner and the pursuit just. If the manner of our pursuit is not right, we may achieve justice yet still be under the influence of the injustice committed against us – the past controlling our present as well as our future.

Conclusion

Gratitude, by its very nature, expresses itself through care and responsible action towards others and nature as a whole. It harbours a moral duty, giving birth to acts marked by a sense of responsibility. The responsibility comes from a recognition of the giftedness of the lives we live and the world we inhabit. In the position of leadership, this means a duty to preserve that which has been passed down to us. Grateful leaders know that they are stewards, not lords. They understand that they are part of a chain, a succession of responsibilities. To be a good steward of the resources means to administer and promote justice. Therefore, a morally well-rounded person or leader has both the virtue of justice and the virtue of gratitude.

The giftedness of life

When we function from a gratitude worldview, acknowledging the good, we are saying and affirming many things. We are recognising the giftedness of life. We realise that we have many things in our lives which are not of our own making. We are acknowledging the contribution of others to our lives and the interconnectedness of human life. We are also acknowledging our limitations and need for others. That brings humility and strengthens our relationships, and influences our attitude towards others.

It is not easy to recognise how much our work or its success depends on others. When our work is a success, we say well done to ourselves. But if we fail, it is easy to look out for someone to blame. The truth is that our work is entirely dependent on others. There is no tangible work product that we can produce without relying on the products and efforts of others. Therefore, any success in our work should lead us to express gratitude to others. The conditions of our work environment could shift from conflict to cooperation as we notice the way the work, not *our* work, gets done – and consequently we practise gratitude.

Conclusion

Let me finish with a story. Whenever Akello returns to his homeland of Uganda, to the countryside where he grew up, he is always struck by the beauty of the natural landscape. Despite a lack of reliable electricity, the welcoming environment makes him hold a deep affection for it. Recently, the area has been blessed with electric power, although the supply remains somewhat unpredictable.

His mornings start early, when he is awakened by a symphony of sounds: birds singing to the dawn, children engaged in playful banter and his grandmother diligently grinding coffee. As he steps outside, he takes a moment to absorb the breathtaking scenery – majestic mountains, beautiful forests, diverse bird species and the rising sun unveiling the beauty covered by the night. In the midst of this mixture of sounds, he discovers a sense of peace and tranquillity, an interconnectedness where each element seems to enhance the beauty of the others. It is the familiar call of his grandmother, summoning him to breakfast, that pulls him from his deep thought.

One evening, as darkness envelops the village and everyone seeks refuge in their homes from the dangers concealed by the night, Akello poses a question to his grandfather. A lifelong teacher, his grandfather is a man of wisdom and spirituality; Akello could listen to him for hours.

'Grandfather,' he calls out, attempting to capture his attention, 'does it not amaze you how the beautiful landscape, with its towering mountains and lush forests, yields so quickly to the impenetrable darkness and transforms into a realm of danger?'

His grandfather responds with a gentle smile and profound wisdom. 'Life, like these surroundings, is full of goodness, Akello. Friendly environments, strong relationships and many blessings. Yet, all these can be overshadowed by a single negative event that consumes your focus. Just as we retreat from the dangers of the night, we often retreat within ourselves when faced with adversity. Bad things with the potential to eclipse all the good around us are

Conclusion

inevitable in this imperfect world. But, as you have observed, when morning comes, the darkness retreats, and the threats of the night lose their grip on our fear.

'The key question is, what is the "morning light" in your life that prevents negativity from obscuring the positive? What inner resource helps you remember that, despite the darkness, you are surrounded by many beautiful and precious things?

'For me, my dear Akello, it is gratitude. Gratitude resists the message of the darkness; it refuses to dwell on what the darkness brings. Instead, it chooses to recognise the enduring goodness of God evident in creation and humanity, the inherent goodness in people despite their flaws, and the goodness within us despite external judgements. Of course, it is the experience of the grace of God that fully awakens the potential for gratitude. However, despite humanity's flaws, inconsistencies and frequent struggles, people have the capacity to approach life with gratitude, recognising and celebrating the abounding goodness that surrounds us. In doing so, we rise above the darkness and its hidden threats, refusing to let it dominate our inner world and rob our civility.'

Afterword

I had just finished singing a selection of songs at a Christian conference in the United Kingdom. I was sitting backstage listening to an onstage interview with a featured speaker. The speaker was Girma Bishaw. As I listened to the interview, I was struck by his authenticity, humility, honesty, clarity and how beautifully he connected with the audience. The following year, at another Christian conference, Girma took time out of his busy schedule to discuss my lecture on the art of lament that he'd heard and how the layers of lament and gratitude are connected. His ideas, insights and perspectives on gratitude were refreshing, and I was thrilled to learn of the book he was writing. Later that year, I reconnected with Girma in New York at a fantastic meeting with African and Caribbean pastors, and leaders from the United Kingdom. I was able to experience Girma in his role as a pastor and as a compelling visionary leader who serves, works, inspires, guides and empowers with integrity. It was powerful.

When Girma graciously invited me to write the afterword for this profound book, I was thrilled and deeply grateful for the opportunity.

As our world continues to be fast-paced and sometimes feels chaotic, I am grateful for the relevance and timing of this book. When we start to feel overwhelmed, Girma's manuscript, with its words pointing us to the gospel of Jesus Christ and how gratitude can keep us rooted and grounded in our faith, is a comforting and reassuring presence. It is a timely reminder of the power of gratitude in our lives, a message that is particularly relevant in today's world.

Girma has shared that gratitude is one of the most powerful divine gifts we can embrace in the human experience. In a society often focused on what is missing, there is a temptation to overlook the transformative act of remembering and valuing what we have already been given. *The Gratitude Way* reminds us that searching, reaching, acknowledging and utilising goodness through gratitude gives opportunities for God to reshape our hearts, perspectives, actions and decisions. Girma's encouragement to us is to practise an ethos of abundance rather than deficiency. The theme of abundance through gratitude can revolutionise our personal lives, relationships with neighbours and people in our communities, and how we see and engage with the world. This transformative power of gratitude is not just a concept but a reality that can inspire hope and resilience.

This book contains inspiring narratives, creative ideas and concepts, keen scholarship, and rich biblical and theological groundwork that guide us to the importance and necessity of gratitude in our lives. Gratitude is a powerful act of worship. It is a form of resistance against sin, evil and darkness. Amid injustice, despair, depression, anxiety, turmoil, suffering and oppression, gratitude can foster hope, rest, endurance, resilience, empathy, peace, spiritual growth and transformation, and it can help us reclaim defiant joy. In a world with seasons and moments of darkness, gratitude can be a radical and stunning light that points us to the Light of the World.

I am deeply thankful to God for the gift of gratitude, for Girma Bishaw and for *The Gratitude Way*. This book, with its inspiring narratives, creative ideas and concepts, keen scholarship and rich biblical and theological groundwork, may well inspire and transform the lives of its readers. I hope you have experienced the profound impact of this book for yourself.

Each breath of life can be a creative, beautiful and transformative act of gratitude.

Ruth Naomi Floyd
Vocalist, Composer, Educator, and Justice Worker, Philadelphia, USA

Appendix 1

Learning to cultivate gratitude – some ideas

1 **Reflect on gratitude:** Begin by contemplating gratitude as a *posture* in life. What does adopting a stance of gratitude mean to you? How might this perspective shift your view of life and yourself, your interactions with others and your approach to challenging situations? Consider the definition of gratitude discussed in this book.
2 **Cultivate gratitude:** Identify ways to incorporate gratitude into your daily routine. Consider the following actions:
   a Reflect on your daily interactions and responses. Did you highlight positive aspects before addressing negatives? What reminders do you need to maintain a gratitude-focused mindset? Each night identify three things that went well and three things for which you are grateful. Record or share these thoughts.
   b Write a gratitude card to someone who has positively impacted your life.
3 **Personal conversation or celebratory events:** Arrange a conversation, meeting or event specifically to express gratitude and celebrate achievements and contributions. (Make expressing gratitude and celebrating achievements a priority in your meetings.)
4 **Personal acknowledgements:** Express appreciation in a personalised way – for example, handwritten thank-you notes saying what you are thankful for; publicly acknowledging a particular person's efforts during meetings or community gatherings.

5. **Gratitude board:** Set up a physical or digital gratitude board or gratitude tree at an event or in your organisation, where members of a community or organisation can post notes of thanks or appreciation for things others have done.
6. **Regular moments of gratitude:** Include moments of gratitude in regular meetings or communications – for example, start meetings by inviting team members to express appreciation for a colleague's contribution or for a positive aspect of their current project.
7. **Social media shout-outs:** Use social media platforms to publicly thank individuals or groups for their contributions to a cause or community, highlighting their specific actions and the positive impact they have had.
8. **Use research to encourage a gratitude culture:** Engage young people in researching acts of kindness and generosity and other positive community stories. Organise an event for them to present their findings, and award the best presentations.
9. **Gratitude Day:** Dedicate a specific day to express gratitude in your family, community or organisation to remind you to cultivate a gratitude posture.
10. **Annual Gratitude Sunday:** Join many other churches that host an annual gratitude service to involve the community in expressing thanks to God and appreciation for individuals. This yearly event helps churches connect with their community and creates opportunities for sharing the gospel. It also allows participants to collectively express gratitude to God for his provision and protection over the United Kingdom, while transforming how we see and relate to one other.

Appendix 2

Learning to cultivate gratitude – discussion topics

1 **Case of Abel and Marinda:** Abel and Marinda have been married for fifteen years. Marinda, known for speaking her mind, said something that deeply hurt Abel. He became increasingly angry and bitter, unable to talk to her or rid himself of negative thoughts. How could gratitude help both Abel and Marinda?
2 **Workplace toxicity:** Sarah faces a toxic work environment, characterised by competition, backbiting and negativity. As a manager, she recognises the need for change in order for the company to thrive. How could gratitude help Sarah foster a more harmonious workplace?
3 **John's reflection:** John, open to learning from mistakes and apologising, talked to his friend Caleb about the lingering effects of the British Empire's wrongs. Initially defensive, John's perspective shifted through Caleb's gratitude approach, starting his conversation by acknowledging the contemporary good in Britain before highlighting the lingering effects of the British Empire's wrongs. How did gratitude help John achieve deep personal reflection?
4 **Community approach:** During a neighbourhood development meeting, Mrs Johnson and others discussed ongoing youth issues, noting past unsuccessful attempts to solve them. A new perspective suggested focusing on the positive contributions of young people instead. How could a gratitude approach benefit this community?

Appendix 3

Case Study: Islington Gratitude Dinner

> 'The impact of the event on the ongoing relationship between the church, public sectors and charities is astounding.'
> Revd Margaret Evans, St Stephen's Canonbury, Islington

Local mission-oriented churches were looking for meaningful connections with their communities and wanting to counter misconceptions of being self-serving. Collaborating with the Gratitude Initiative, Islington church leaders chose gratitude as a means to acknowledge and appreciate the services of public-sector workers and charities. The church leaders recognised that there were various platforms where they could express their concerns and encourage dialogue for the betterment of their services, but there were few opportunities to appreciate positive contributions.

In March 2018, local churches joined forces to host a Gratitude Dinner, inviting community representatives. The event's success sparked enthusiasm for a follow-up. Consequently, in February 2020, they organised a more formal Gratitude Dinner. This time, the guest list was expanded to include teachers, doctors, nurses, cleaners, ambulance staff, firefighters, police, council members, greenspace and other municipal workers, and representatives from ten local charities.

The event, attended by 133 guests and church leaders, surpassed all expectations. By the end of the evening, there was unanimous agreement that it should become an annual event to nurture a culture of gratitude in Islington. The impact on relationships between the Church and public sectors has been remarkable, underscoring its transformational potential.

I include this example to show that there are tangible things we can do to demonstrate and promote gratitude in our communities. A meal and a word of thanks is just one form it can take. I hope that the responses below inspire you to step out and find a way to bring the hope of gratitude to the people around you.

Responses

'We would like to thank you and all your colleagues for the lovely certificate you awarded us. It is not often that we are recognised for our work, and your award meant so much to each of us, showing that the public appreciates and cares about our role in the community.'
London Ambulance Service, Islington branch

'Our project, working with homeless and marginalised people, is not glamorous and we do not generally seek publicity because many of our clients prefer to be anonymous. So, it was heartening that local leaders and the Gratitude Initiative noticed us and showed appreciation. We feel encouraged and even more determined to fulfil our mission of justice and support for those on the edge of society.'
Manna Charity for the Homeless

Welcoming speech at the second Islington Gratitude Dinner (2020)

We are delighted that you have come to our second Islington Gratitude Dinner evening.

We believe that it is appropriate to create a platform where we appreciate and thank you for the services we have received over the years and for what you mean to our communities.

We are grateful!

If we take a problem-orientated approach to the development of our communities, starting with the problems and difficulties, we only enhance a blame culture, pointing the finger at those responsible, and that blinds us from recognising and growing the strengths of our communities.

The concept of gratitude, on the other hand, shows us that community is built by celebrating our strengths and, together, telling the stories so much that those strengths become normal for us. They become the formative narrative that energises us to engage with our problems in a constructive manner.

So, to be grateful is to pause from the activity of life, to consider the good around us and give it due recognition and acknowledgement. In the process, we transform our perspective, our conversation and our community.

Therefore, today we want to appreciate and celebrate you: your commitment, your consistency, your hard work, your availability and your compassion. For being there in the time of our need.

We believe that you are the strength and jewel of our community.

Between you all, you inspire, you educate, you rescue, you give comfort, you serve, you provide, you lead, you counsel, you intervene, you represent, you defend and you are a voice for the voiceless.

You do all this, at times, risking your own life and well-being.

Thank you for your readiness to help.

Thank you for your willingness to take a risk to save others in the face of danger.

Thank you for your hard work and availability.

Thank you for doing your work with a sense of duty and commitment.

Thank you! Thank you! Thank you! Thank you!

Poem

A framed copy of this poem was given to representatives of the public and voluntary sector workers of Islington.

Thank you
Your presence makes us feel safe
Serving others comes to you at a great cost
Your courage in the face of danger is selfless
Your compassion and care make us feel at ease
and comfortable even when we are in pain
It is to you we turn to when we feel threatened,
unsafe and in danger
Your hospitality, service and support help us to be effective in
what we do
Your wisdom and dedication prepare our young ones for life
You make our community environmentally friendly
Your generosity, kindness and love change many lives
You are consistent in what you do
We just want you to know that you have made
and continue to make a difference in our society
For that, we are utterly grateful.

Further reading

Bass, Diana Butler, *Grateful: The Transformative Power of Giving Thanks* (HarperOne, 2018)
Cooperrider, David L., Diana K. Whitney and Jacqueline M. Stavros, *The Appreciative Inquiry Handbook: For Leaders of Change* (Berrett-Koehler Publishers, 2008)
Dargin, Star Sargent, *Leading with Gratitude: 21st Century Solutions to Boost Engagement and Innovation* (Pleasant Vines Publishing, 2018)
Donati, Pierpaolo, *Relational Sociology: A New Paradigm for the Social Sciences: Ontological Explorations* (Taylor and Francis, 2011)
Emmons, Robert A. and Michael E. McCullough (eds), *The Psychology of Gratitude* (Oxford University Press, 2004)
Engels, Jeremy David, *The Art of Gratitude* (State University of New York Press, 2018)
Froh, Jeffrey and Giacomo Bono, *Making Grateful Kids: The science of building character* (Templeton Foundation Press, 2015)
Siddiqui Mona and Nathanael Vette (eds), *A Theology of Gratitude: Christian and Muslim Perspectives* (Cambridge University Press, 2022)

Gratitude Initiative website: https://gratitudeinitiative.org.uk

Notes

2 Why gratitude and why now?

1 Chimamanda Ngozi Adichie, 'The Danger of a Single Story', TED talk, July 2009.
2 Girma Bishaw, 'Gratitude as an Approach to Intercultural Engagement: Exploring the introduction and embodiment of gratitude as an approach to intercultural engagement between the diaspora and native Christian leaders in London', Asbury Theological Seminary, April 2019, available at: https://place.asburyseminary.edu/cgi/viewcontent.cgi?article=2413&context=ecommonsatsdissertations (accessed June 2025).
3 For example, the story of the woman caught in adultery and her accusers (John 8:1–11) and the story of Jesus being anointed, according to the Pharisees, 'by a sinful woman' (Luke 7:36–50).
4 Alistair Begg, *Preaching for God's Glory* (Crossway Books, 1999), 23.
5 Martin Luther King Jr, 'Loving Your Enemies', sermon, Dexter Avenue Baptist Church, 17 November 1957.
6 Afua Hirsch, 'The scramble for Africa has moved on, but Britain hasn't', *The Guardian*, 4 September 2018, available at: https://www.theguardian.com/commentisfree/2018/sep/04/africa-britain-trade-theresa-may-brexit (accessed June 2025).
7 Alan Paton, *Cry, the Beloved Country* (Jonathan Cape, 1940), 26.
8 Peter Block, *Community: The Structure of Belonging* (Berrett-Koehler Publishers, 2009), 15.

3 Gratitude explored

1 Robert A. Emmons, *Thanks! How the New Science of Gratitude Can Make You Happier* (Houghton Mifflin Harcourt, 2007).
2 Robert A. Emmons and Michael E. McCullough (eds), *The Psychology of Gratitude* (Oxford University Press, 2004), 10.

Notes

3 Robert C. Solomon, *The Passions: The Myth and Nature of Human Emotions* (Anchor Books, 1977), 316.
4 D. B. Harned, *Patience: How We Wait upon the World* (Cowley, 1997), 175.
5 Solomon, *The Passions*. P. A. Bertocci and R. M. Millard, *Personality and the Good: Psychological and Ethical Perspective* (David McKay, 1963), 389.
6 Alex Wood, Greater Good Gratitude Summit in California, September 2014. Jeremy David Engels, *The Art of Gratitude* (State University of New York Press, 2018), 1. Christopher Hedges, *Empire of Illusion: The End of Literacy and the Triumph of the Spectacle* (Nation Books, 2009), 122. Fred Berger, 'Gratitude', *Ethics* 85 (1975): 298–309. Atif Khalil, 'When Does a Virtue Become a Vice? Gratitude as panacea and poison in Sufi ethics' in Mona Siddiqui and Nathanael Vette (eds), *A Theology of Gratitude: Christian and Muslim Perspectives* (Cambridge University Press, 2022), 51–57.
7 S. H. Webb, *The Gifting God: A Trinitarian Ethics of Excess* (OUP, 1996), 49.
8 For example, David Shariatmadari, 'Could gratitude be the most important emotion of all?', *The Guardian*, 30 October 2015, https://www.theguardian.com/commentisfree/2015/oct/30/gratitude-most-important-emotion. Alex Wood, Stephen Joseph and Alex Linley, 'Gratitude: Parent of all virtues', *The Psychologist* vol. 20, January 2007, https://thepsychologist.bps.org.uk/volume-20/edition-1/gratitude-parent-all-virtues (accessed June 2025).
9 In theological terms, this could be described as being the natural, existential or ontological response.
10 By 'the Fall', we refer to humanity's disobedience and the resulting separation from God, as depicted in the Genesis story.
11 Matthew 22:37–39; Mark 12:30–31.
12 This does not mean that one should stay in an abusive situation, endure the abuse or feel grateful for it. Instead, it pertains to the recovery process. The devastation of abuse lies in its psychological impact, often causing us to be defined by the abusive experience. Here, gratitude becomes valuable, reminding us of our beauty,

qualities, strength and talents. It helps us avoid being defined or distracted by the abuse, allowing us to live the rest of our lives more fully.

13 Miroslav Volf is the author of many books, including *Exclusion and Embrace: A theological exploration of identity* (Abingdon Press, 1996). This conversation took place at the launch of the Gratitude Initiative, St Paul's Cathedral, London, 28 November 2020 (lightly edited).

4 Gratitude misunderstood

1 Chloe Carmichael, 'What is Toxic Positivity?', *Psychology Today*, 1 July 2021, https://www.psychologytoday.com/us/blog/the-high-functioning-hotspot/202107/what-is-toxic-positivity (accessed June 2025). Whitney Goodman, *Toxic Positivity: Keeping It Real in a World Obsessed with Being Happy* (Orion Spring, 2022).

2 Harvey C. Kwiyani is CEO of Global Connections, Founder and Executive Director of Missio Africanus, lecturer at Church Mission Society in Oxford and author of many books, including *Multicultural Kingdom: Ethnic Diversity, Mission and the Church* (SCM Press, 2020).

5 The biblical and theological foundation of the gratitude way

1 Dong-Hee Sohn, *My Cup Overflows: The Life and Martyrdom of Reverend Yang-Won Sohn* (Christian Literature Crusade, 2001).

2 This is a repeated refrain in Genesis 1 – in verses 10, 12, 18, 21, 25. In Genesis 1:31, we read 'God saw all that he had made, and it was very good.'

3 Gordon D. Fee, *The First Epistle to the Corinthians* (William B. Eerdmans, 2014), 185.

4 F. F. Bruce, *1 and 2 Corinthians* (Eerdmans, 1980), 49.

5 Fee, *First Epistle to the Corinthians*, 186.

6 Fee, *First Epistle to the Corinthians*, 186.

7 C. K. Barrett, *A Commentary on the First Epistle to the Corinthians* (Edinburgh: T&T Clark, 1991), 36.

8 Bruce, *1 and 2 Corinthians*, 20.

Notes

9 Paul addresses marriage and celibacy (7:1–16), food offered to idols (8:1–10), order in conducting public worship and exercising spiritual gifts (1 Corinthians 12 – 14), and the rising of the dead (15:1–22).
10 Leon Morris, *1 Corinthians* (InterVarsity Press, 1985), 37.
11 Morris, *1 Corinthians*, 37.
12 Richard B. Hays, *First Corinthians* (John Knox Press, 1997), 20.
13 Fee, *First Epistle to the Corinthians*, 36.
14 Fee, *First Epistle to the Corinthians*, 37.
15 Hays, *First Corinthians*, 17.
16 Morris, *1 Corinthians*, 65.
17 Internal danger refers to threats that emerge and operate within the Church, leading to deception and the introduction of practices that contradict the teachings and character of Christ. In contrast, external danger consists of persecution and threats that originate from outside the Church. Jurgen Roloff, *Revelation* (Fortress Press, 1993), 54.
18 Roloff, *Revelation*, 61.
19 Christopher J. H. Wright, *The Message of Jeremiah Against Wind and Tide* (IVP, 2014), 292–93.
20 Wright, *Jeremiah*, 292–93.
21 Wright, *Jeremiah*, 292–93.
22 Bruce, *1 and 2 Corinthians*, 328.
23 Morris, *1 Corinthians*, 68.
24 Morris, *1 Corinthians*, 44.
25 Bruce, *1 and 2 Corinthians*, 321.
26 Barrett, *First Epistle to the Corinthians*, 490.
27 Paul S. Fiddes, *Participating in God: A Pastoral Doctrine of the Trinity* (Westminster John Knox Press, 2000), 50.
28 Liturgy is the order of the church worship service including the confession, prayers and thanksgiving. We pray and approach God the Father in the name of Christ the Son, by the power of the Holy Spirit.
29 Fee, *First Epistle to the Corinthians*, 583.
30 Barrett, *First Epistle to the Corinthians*, 284.
31 Barrett, *First Epistle to the Corinthians*, 287.
32 Craig S. Keener, *1–2 Corinthians* (CUP, 2005), 104.

33 Roloff, *Revelation*, 80.
34 Elisabeth S. Fiorenza, *Revelation: Vision of a Just World* (Fortress Press, 1991), 60.
35 J. Ziesler, *Paul's Letter to the Romans* (SCM, 1989), 77.
36 John Stott, *The Message of Romans* (IVP, 1994), 72.
37 I. H. Marshall, *The Pastoral Epistles* (T&T Clark, 2006), 158.
38 William D. Mounce, *Pastoral Epistle* (Zondervan, 2000), 544.
39 Michael Wilcock, *The Message of Luke* (IVP, 1997), 166.
40 Norval Geldenhuys, *Commentary on the Gospel of Luke* (Marshall, Morgan & Scott, 1950), 436.

6 Gratitude and social change

1 For example, John Ashmore, 'Government launches new £50m fund to promote integration and "British values"', PoliticsHome, 13 March 2018, https://www.politicshome.com/news/article/government-launches-new-50m-fund-to-promote-integration-and-british-values (accessed June 2025).
2 For example, Remembrance Sunday, and the King's official birthday with the Trooping of the Colour – or even Bonfire Night! (I am actually surprised by how few national celebrations we have in the UK – perhaps it would be good to have a few more.)
3 Passover (Pesach) – Leviticus 23:5; Feast of Unleavened Bread (Matzot) – Leviticus 23:6–8; Feast of Firstfruits (Bikkurim) – Leviticus 23:10–14; Feast of Weeks (Shavuot or Pentecost) – Leviticus 23:15–21; Feast of Trumpets (Rosh Hashanah) – Leviticus 23:24–25; Day of Atonement (Yom Kippur) – Leviticus 23:27–32; Feast of Tabernacles (Sukkot) – Leviticus 23:34–43.
4 Emiliana Mangone, 'Gratitude and the Relational Theory of Society', *Human Areas* 2 (2019), 34–44, https://doi.org/10.1007/s42087-018-0040-8 (accessed June 2025).
5 Pierpaolo Donati, *Relational Sociology: A new paradigm for the social sciences* (Routledge, 2011), Kindle Location 109.
6 Appreciative Inquiry has been used with a wide variety of governmental and non-profit organisations including the US Navy, the United Nations and many more business and

non-profit organisations such as HR professionals, professional life coaches, change management consultants and social workers. 'Appreciate Inquiry by Industry', Champlain College, 2024, https://appreciativeinquiry.champlain.edu/by-sector (accessed June 2025).
7 Theodore Kinni, ' The Art of Appreciative Inquiry', Harvard Business School, 22 September 2023, https://hbswk.hbs.edu/archive/the-art-of-appreciative-inquiry (accessed June 2025).
8 David Cooperrider and Suresh Srivastva, 'Appreciative Inquiry in Organizational Life' in R. W. Woodman and W. A. Pasmore (eds), *Research in Organizational Change and Development* vol. 1 (JAI Press, 1987), 129–69, available at: https://www.researchgate.net/publication/265225217_Appreciative_Inquiry_in_Organizational_Life (accessed June 2025).
9 For example, Diana Whitney, Corporation for Positive Change and Saybrook Graduate School and Research Center, and Jacqueline M. Stavros, EDM Lawrence Technological University College of Management.
10 Greg Banaga Jr, 'A Spiritual Path to Organizational Renewal: the Christian spiritual dimension of AI, an essay' in S. A. Hammond and C. Royal (eds), *Lessons from the Field: Applying Appreciative Inquiry* (Practical Press, 1998).
11 Andy Frost is Director at Share Jesus International, Chair at Mission Collective, Joint CEO for Gather Movement and the author of many books, including *Long Story Short: Finding Your Place in God's Unfolding Story* (SPCK, 2018). This is a lightly edited extract from his presentation at the Gratitude Initiative Summit in 2022.

7 The benefits of gratitude

1 Martin Heidegger, *What is Called Thinking?*, trans. J. Glenn Gray (Harper Perennial, 2004).
2 Heidegger, *What is Called Thinking?*
3 Rick A. Furtak, *Wisdom in Love: Kierkegaard and the Ancient Quest for Emotional Integrity* (University of Notre Dame Press, 2005).
4 David Levinson, James J. Ponzetti Jr and Peter F. Jorgensen (eds), *Encyclopedia of Human Emotions* (Macmillan, 1999). T. Dalgleish

and M. J. Power (eds), *Handbook of Cognition and Emotion* (Wiley, 1999).
5 Martin Seligman and Mihaly Csikszentmihalyi, 'Positive Psychology: An introduction', *American Psychologist* 55, no. 1 (2000): 5–14.
6 F. Sirois, 'Wall of Gratitude could help to improve mental health and wellbeing', University of Sheffield, 7 September 2018.
7 Dr Fuschia M. Sirois is author of *Procrastination: What It Is, Why It's a Problem, and What You Can Do About It* (American Psychological Association, 2022). The conversation is lightly edited. One section of her website focuses on the area of gratitude: https://fuschiasirois.com/positive-psychology/#Gratitude (accessed June 2025).
8 'Wall of Gratitude will highlight what Sheffield is grateful for', *The Star*, 19 September 2018, https://www.thestar.co.uk/news/wall-of-gratitude-will-highlight-what-sheffield-is-grateful-for-432822 (accessed June 2025).

Conclusion

1 John Barnes, *The Uncomfortable Truth about Racism* (Headline Publishing Group, 2021).
2 Barnes, *Uncomfortable Truth about Racism*, 210.

www.ingramcontent.com/pod-product-compliance
Lightning Source LLC
Chambersburg PA
CBHW060353110426
42743CB00036B/2902